THE TRANSFORMATIVE POWER OF THE 3 C'S

GROWING COMPASSION, CREATIVITY & CONNECTION

BILL C. MYERS

Red Cardinals Flight
Publishing

Library of Congress Control Number: 2024922953

Hardcover ISBN: 978-1-965193-02-0
Paperback ISBN: 978-1-965193-01-3
Ebook ISBN: 978-1-965193-00-6

Published by: Red Cardinals Flight Publishing 5534 Saint Joe Road Fort Wayne, IN 46835

Editor: Dr. Ruth L. Baskerville
www.wwexcellence.org

Cover Design: Miblart

First Edition: 2024

Printed in the United States of America

For information about speaking engagements, coaching, or bulk purchases, please contact: www.billcmyers.com

I dedicate this book to the loving memory of:

Gloria Myers

Jack

Donnie Harris

Ellie Sellars

Luke Perry

Robbie McNeill

They were all celestial lights whose radiance touched countless lives, including my own. Although they have journeyed beyond our earthly realm, their wisdom, love, and boundless creativity continue to illuminate the paths of generations, inspiring us all to embrace compassion, nurture connections, and unleash our creative spirits. This is a testament to the eternal brilliance of their souls.

ACKNOWLEDGMENTS

As I stand at the shore of gratitude, gazing upon the vast ocean of influences that have shaped this work, I find myself in awe of its depth and breadth. This philosophical framework, cultivated from the very dawn of my existence, has been nourished by countless individuals, each contributing a precious drop to this expansive sea of wisdom and experience.

To attempt a brief acknowledgment feels akin to capturing the essence of an ocean in a single shell – a task both daunting and humbling. Yet, I feel compelled to honor each contributor by name, for every drop creates a ripple, and these ripples have coalesced into the waves that have carried me to this moment of profound growth, reflection, and gratitude.

It is with a full heart that I acknowledge those who have been instrumental in bringing this work to life, recognizing that their influence extends far beyond these pages, creating ever-expanding circles of compassion, creativity, and connection.

Family and Personal Relationships: First and foremost, I extend my deepest gratitude to my parents, Georgia and Bill Myers. Your unwavering love, steadfast belief in me, and constant inspiration have been the foundation upon which this book---and indeed, my life's journey---has been built. To my sisters, Crystal and Robbin, my niece Jacque, and my brother Kenny Dixon: your encouragement and support have been a constant source of strength. I extend my gratitude to my uncles Claud and Mike, affectionately known as

'Those Myers Boys,' and my dear Aunt Marva. Your lives have exemplified how to make the most of one's innate abilities, serving as an inspiring model for me. I owe an immeasurable debt of gratitude to my grandparents, Erma & William M.S. Myers. Your eternal guidance continues to move me in new and beautiful ways.

To my first love, Kelly Evans Johnson: Your presence in my life has been a beautiful testament to the enduring power of genuine connection and a constant reminder that love is forever.

To my second mother, Susie Dartis, and my brothers Mark and Ritchie, and sister Terry, I thank you for teaching me that family is not only defined by blood.

I am profoundly grateful to my dear friend and confidante, Kathy Jordan, for always being there. Thanks to my sister and longtime colleague, Lapacazo Sandoval for being my morning coffee clutch partner. A special thank you to Vivi Spaulding for your encouragement and assistance with my caregiver responsibilities has allowed me the space and time to pour myself into this work. Thanks to CareForth for all your support in my caregiving responsibilities.

Writing Mentors: I am indebted to the many professionals who encouraged me to share my voice and write this book, including Markette Sheppard, Hallie Bryant, and my creative writing teacher, Diana Ensign. A special thank you to Mike Lamm, Richard Brendan and Nathaniel Hankerson for your unwavering belief in my talent. I'm also profoundly grateful to Betsy Blankenbaker for encouraging me to write and for reminding me that this is my story to tell.

Theatre Tribe: My heart is full of appreciation for my dear friends and colleagues in the professional theatre including LaChanze, Julia Lema, Roz Ryan, Don Scardino & my beloved Godspell Family, Joseph Papp & the Public Theatre, Playwrights Horizons, Lynn Ahrens and Steve Flaherty, Hal Prince, John Kander and Chita Rivera for their profound impact on my theatrical journey. I also want to express my gratitude to the Indianapolis Theatre community: Ellie Sellers, Bill Goodman,

Angela Brown, Ellen Kingston, Tony Tooley, Jo Read Trakimas, and countless others. Special thanks to Footlite Musicals, Jean Cones, Bryan Fonseca, Sandra Gay, Ron Spencer, Helen Whitelowe, Constance Macy and Janet Allen. A special note of gratitude to David Neighbors for challenging me to grow and introducing me to the works of Stephen Sondheim.

Music Tribe: To my family of professional musicians including Les "Bear" Taylor, Jimmy Coe, Pookie Johnson, Russell Webster, Slide Hampton and the Hampton Family, Rudy Finnell, Jimmy Guilford, Count Fisher, Clifford Ratliff, Cynthia Layne, Kelleen Strutz, Brenda Williams, Sandy Lomax, and Turk Burke: your music, mentorship, and support have shaped my journey. Thanks to brother Brad Guinn & my good friends at Fame Studios in Muscle Shoals. A special shout-out to my BMTC Music brothers Larry Sledge, Robert Coleman, Darnell Lark & Richard Hart. I would also like to acknowledge Ralph Adams, David Andrichik, and David Allee for their role in preserving the Indianapolis Jazz Legacy.

Faith Community: Thank you to all my fellow members of the clergy. I am deeply grateful to my teacher and renowned author on compassion, Matthew Fox. To the University of Metaphysics and the leadership of Dr. Paul Leon Masters, and fellow metaphysician, Dr. Linda Salvin: your spiritual guidance and shared commitment to metaphysical understanding is truly inspiring.

Community Leaders: To Deputy Mayor Judith Thomas and Mayor Joe Hogsett: Your commitment to progress and positive change in the City of Indianapolis has been truly inspiring. A special acknowledgment to Yvette Reid for your tireless efforts in making a positive difference and significant cultural contribution in the lives of the good people of Barbados.

Podcast Guests and Media Collaborators: To Christine McIver and the team at Inspired Choices Network, I want to thank you for providing a platform for important conversations on racism and social justice in America. I am grateful to all those who shared their time and expertise on my Bill Myers Inspires podcast, including Rep. Justin J. Pearson, Tim Guinee, Macy Gray, Sharon Leslie Morgan, U.S. Congressman André Carson, Jennifer Jones Austin, Dr. John Dorhauer, Marianna Van Zeller, Stanley Nelson, Janus Adams, and Jeffery Robinson.

Book Team and Professional Support: A special note of thanks goes to Dr. Ruth Baskerville for her exceptional editing skills and infinite patience, Miblart for their beautiful design work, Kati Taylor for her expertise in website design and social media management, and Antonio Toppin for his wonderful photographs. Thanks to my good friend and right-hand Scot McKim for the ripple and steadfast support through the process.

To the Helen Wells Agency, including Helen, Lori Fetter & Nancy Bastian: thank you for your continued support and love.

Service Organizations: To Optimist International and Paula Reiling: thank you for your commitment to promoting optimism as a way of life. To The Ronald McDonald House and Pam Anderson: your dedication to supporting families in times of need is truly inspiring.

Social Justice Institutions: To Coming to the Table and my good friend Thomas Norman DeWolf: thank you for your years of service in creating spaces dedicated to racial healing and reconciliation. To Allen Jones, my co-facilitator of the Coming to The Table National Virtual Group: thank you for your partnership in this important work. A special thanks to Fran Sutton-Williams and Dixon D. White for your tireless work as unapologetic warriors in the fight for social justice.

Arts and Cultural Institutions: I extend my heartfelt thanks to The Indianapolis Museum of Art, Maxwell Anderson, Bezie Blickenstaff, and Linda Duke for providing me the opportunity to find my voice and honor my favorite American figure, the Rev. Dr. Martin Luther King, Jr. I'm also deeply grateful to Dr. Tyron Cooper and The Archives of African American Music & Culture, Michelle Materre and

Women Make Movies for their invaluable work in preserving and promoting diverse voices. A special acknowledgment to the African American Jazz Caucus and mentors Dr. Larry Ridley, Anderson White, Dr. Billy Taylor, Dr. David Baker, Dr. Willis Kirk and Rev. Marvin Chandler for their significant contributions to jazz education and the preservation of its rich history.

Broad Ripple Rockets and Early Influences: A special shout-out to all my fellow Broad Ripple Rockets: our shared experiences and the spirit of our alma mater continue to influence and inspire me.

Thank you to my brother Bruce Buchanan, and Jack Hogan in our shared interest in connection and uniting the divide.

I thank God for each and every one of you. To God be the glory!

I am filled with awe and wonder at the countless drops of wisdom poured into me by each person named here and many more unnamed. These individual contributions have coalesced into a mighty wave in the vast ocean of human understanding, carrying this book to shore. I marvel at how each seemingly small act of kindness, each word of encouragement, each moment of shared insight has contributed to this work. Now, as this book ventures forth, may it create its own ripples of compassion, creativity, and connection, touching lives in ways yet unimagined.

With profound gratitude,

Bill C. Myers

INTRODUCTION
THE SHOWSTOPPER WITHIN

Life, in all its complexity and wonder, is the "greatest show on earth!" And you, dear reader, are its star performer. But like any memorable production, life requires direction, creativity, and a touch of magic to truly shine. This is where our journey begins.

I've always been fascinated by the power of performance to change hearts and minds. This fascination was sparked early in my life and influenced by my father's innovative community work and my own journey through the entertainment industry. These early experiences showed me how compassion, creativity, and connection could bridge divides and touch lives in profound ways.

When my father bought me a trumpet, he unknowingly set me on a path that would weave through show business to social justice and ultimately to this book. That shiny brass instrument became my gateway to understanding the profound impact of creativity and connection. I still recall the moment I first heard Louis Armstrong play. It wasn't just music; it was a revelation. In that instant, I understood that creativity could speak to the soul in a language more profound than words.

These experiences taught me that compassion, creativity, and connection -- what I call the "3 C's" -- are not just abstract concepts. They are powerful tools for personal transformation and societal change. Throughout this book, we'll explore how these principles can enhance every aspect of your life, from your relationships to your career and personal fulfillment.

Throughout my years in the entertainment world, I've learned that growth and learning are most powerful when they're also engaging and fun. So, I've decided to bring a touch of that showbiz magic to our adventure. As we transition between chapters, you'll notice we're treating this journey like the production of a lifetime - with you as the star! These playful interludes are more than just fun; they're designed to help you anticipate and remember key themes in a unique way, much like how a memorable performance can leave lasting impressions.

In the pages that follow, you'll explore how to cultivate deep compassion, not just for others but for yourself. We'll unlock the creative potential that resides within you, waiting to be expressed. And we'll discover how to forge authentic connections that enrich your life and ripple out to touch countless others.

This book isn't just about personal development; it's about becoming the director of your own life's story. It's about turning everyday moments into standing ovations and turning challenges into award-winning performances. We'll delve into real-life stories, scientific research, and practical exercises that will help you embody the 3 C's in your daily life.

I'm reminded of my own formative years at *Broad Ripple High School* in Indianapolis. It's not lost on me that the word "Ripple" was part of my educational foundation, especially as we explore the ripple effects of compassion, creativity, and connection in this book. Our school's motto, "Broader, Stronger, Richer," seems almost prophetic now, reflecting the very essence of personal growth.

I don't believe it's a coincidence that this school, which emphasized the humanities and nurtured creativity, played a significant role in shaping my perspective. It's where I began to see the broader implications of the 3 C's in action. And I'm proud to share this alma mater with none other than David Letterman. Yes, I'm a "Broad Ripple Rocket" for life, and that spirit of reaching for the stars infuses every page of this book.

In this grand production we call life, you're not just the star -- you're the writer, director, and producer too. Each chapter will build upon the last, providing you with the tools and insights you need to create a life masterpiece that's broader, stronger, and richer in every sense.

So, get ready to step into the spotlight. Whether you're looking to enhance your personal relationships, boost your professional success, or simply live a more fulfilling life, the 3 C's will guide you every step of the way.

Lights, camera, action - let's begin the transformative journey of the 3 C's! Remember, the show of your life is about to begin, and it's going to be spectacular. Turn the page, and let the adventure unfold.

CONTENTS

1

THE 3 C'S REVOLUTION

"Compassion, creativity, and connection are the three great forces that drive human progress."
— Dalai Lama

As he gazed beyond the realm of the living, Steve Jobs, visionary co-founder of *Apple*, reportedly uttered his last words: *"Oh wow. Oh wow. Oh, wow."* What did he see in those last moments that inspired such awe? While we can't know for certain, his words remind us of the profound wonder that life can offer — a wonder we often overlook in our daily rush. In the twilight of his life, this titan of innovation came to a profound realization.

> *"I have reached the pinnacle of success in business,"* he reflected. *"In other people's eyes, my life is a success. However, aside from work, I've had little joy."*

Jobs' poignant reflection reminds us that it's not the watch on our wrist or the car in our driveway that matters, but the lives we've touched, the love we've shared, and the positive change we've created in the world.

> *These three elements – compassion, creativity, and connection*
> *– form the cornerstone of a truly fulfilled life, and they are*
> *the keys to unlocking our full potential as human beings.*

Let's consider how cultivating these "3 C's" can transform, not just our own lives, but the world around us, leading to a life of genuine happiness and meaningful success far beyond the shallow metrics of wealth and status.

While the power of the 3 C's is universal, my journey to discovering their transformative impact was deeply personal.

From Spark to Flame: My 3 C's Awakening

In the early spring of 1966, as the *Civil Rights Movement* reached a fever pitch across America, I entered the world in Indianapolis, Indiana. Born to a White mother and a Black father, I straddled two worlds from my first breath. Our family was a living embodiment of the change sweeping the nation—a change that many welcomed but others fiercely resisted. Little did I know then that this unique position, often fraught with challenges, would become the fertile ground from which a transformative philosophy would grow.

From my earliest memories, examples of compassion, creativity, and connection surrounded me, though I didn't recognize them as such until much later in life. The fabric of my family's legacy of service, resilience, and bridge-building exemplified these principles, which I now refer to as the 3 C's.

On Compassion

On a crisp autumn morning in 1977, I found myself perched on a hard wooden chair in my grandfather's basement office. The room smelled of old books and the faint metallic scent of his trusted *Smith Corona* typewriter. I had come to him with a simple request of a five-dollar loan. What followed was a lesson in compassion and responsibility that would shape my understanding of both for years to come.

> *"Billy,"* he began, his voice deep and measured. *"You want to borrow five dollars? You want to borrow five dollars from your Granddad? Let's talk about this, fella."*

For the next two hours, my grandfather unraveled the concept of loans, savings, and financial responsibility. But it wasn't just a lecture on money. It was a masterclass in compassionate teaching.

As he wrapped up, I watched him pull out his wallet and, with his always immaculate and manicured hands, he reached in, pulling out a crisp, new five-dollar bill from his wallet. *"I'm going to loan you five dollars,"* he said, *"but I want it back the same way I gave it to you."*

Over the next week, I learned the true depth of his lesson. My initial attempts to repay him — first with a mix of coins and crumpled bills, then with five ones — were met with silent rejection. It wasn't until I returned with a crisp, new five-dollar bill that he accepted the repayment.

This experience, which I'll explore further in Chapter 3, was my first profound lesson in the power of compassion. My grandfather's patience, his willingness to invest time in teaching me, and his gentle, but firm approach showed me that genuine compassion goes beyond mere kindness. It involves empowering others, holding them to high standards, and guiding them toward growth.

On Creativity

The dusty beams of afternoon sunlight filtered through our living room window, illuminating specks of dust that danced in the air. I sat cross-legged on the carpet, my six-year-old eyes glued to our black-and-white television set. It was a Saturday, and as the morning cartoons gave way to the afternoon movie, little did I know that I was about to encounter a moment that would change my life.

The movie was *The Five Pennies,* starring Danny Kaye. It was a biopic about jazz cornetist Red Nichols. But it wasn't Nichols who captured my attention. It was a supporting character, an older Black man whose presence seemed to fill the screen. When he lifted his trumpet to his lips, the world around me faded away. The joy, the energy, and the sheer life in his playing struck a chord deep within me.

As the credits rolled, I leaped to my feet, my heart pounding with excitement. "Mom! Mom!" I shouted, racing to find her. "I know what I want to do with my life!" My mother's laughter was tinged with affection as she asked, *"Oh really? What's that?"* "I want to play the trumpet!" I declared, with all the confidence of the cosmos.

Her curiosity piqued, *"And why do you want to play the trumpet?"* My response was simple but profound: "Because I want to make other people feel the way he made me feel." That "he," I would later learn, was the legendary Louis Armstrong. And the feeling he inspired in me — a feeling I couldn't articulate then but now recognize as pure joy — became my driving force.

I didn't realize then how this moment would shape my understanding of creativity, a concept we'll explore further in **Chapter 6**. It taught me that creativity isn't just about making something new; it's about touching hearts, inspiring emotions, and connecting with others on a profound level.

On Connection

The school gymnasium buzzed with excitement as hundreds of children filed in, their chatter reverberating off the high ceilings. I sat among them, my heart pounding with anticipation and nervousness. Today was the day of the annual *Officer Friendly* presentation by the *Indianapolis Police Department,* and my father was the star of the show.

As he walked onto the stage in his crisp police uniform, the crowd fell silent. But it wasn't his glistening gold badge, his fully rigged gun belt, complete with handcuffs, his shiny black patent leather shoes, or his authoritative presence that commanded attention. No, it was the warmth of his smile and the whimsical twinkle in his eye that drew everyone in.

 "Good morning, boys and girls!" he boomed enthusiastically. *"Who's ready for some magic?"*

A chorus of cheers erupted. I watched in awe as my father, a respected police officer and someone I knew as "Daddy" at home transformed into a captivating performer. He pulled colorful scarves out of thin air and made coins disappear and reappear, all while weaving in important lessons about safety and trust.

But the real magic wasn't in the tricks. It was in the connection my father forged with his audience. I saw it in the wide-eyed wonder of my classmates, in their eager hands shooting up to volunteer, in their rapt attention as he spoke about seeing police officers as friends and protectors.

This experience laid the foundation for my understanding of connection, a principle that would guide my career and which I'll examine in **Chapter 4** when we explore how authentic relationships can fuel our compassion and creativity, creating a positive cycle of growth and connection.

Every day I spent with my grandfather, he would always say, *"You learn something every day."* These words were like seeds planted in fertile soil, growing over time to shape my understanding of the world and my place within it.

My mother, too, played a pivotal role in this journey. Her encouragement to pursue spiritual growth and development opened my eyes to the vast landscapes within us all. It's a pursuit that has no end, requiring an internal exploration of the self and the soul on a constant quest to discover what it means to be genuinely connected to ourselves, others, and the world around us.

As I reflect on these formative experiences — my grandfather's compassionate lesson, the creative spark ignited by Louis Armstrong, and my father's masterful demonstration of connection — I saw how they shaped my understanding of what I now call the 3 C's: *Compassion, Creativity,* and *Connection.*

These principles are more than just abstract concepts. They are powerful tools for personal growth, community building, and social change within our daily lives and our professional endeavors, as we create a more just and equitable world.

We'll delve into the science behind these concepts, examining how compassion rewires our brains, how creativity drives innovation and problem-solving, and how genuine connections can transform communities. We'll look at real-world examples of the 3 C's in action, from grassroots community initiatives to global movements for change.

Most importantly, we'll explore practical strategies for incorporating the 3 C's into your life. Whether you're a business leader looking to build a more innovative and empathetic workplace, or an educator seeking to connect more deeply with your students, or someone who wants to make a positive impact in your community, the principles of compassion, creativity, and connection can guide you toward more fulfilling and impactful actions.

My journey from a biracial child in 1960s Indianapolis to a professional musician, actor, life coach, minister, civic leader, and advocate for social justice is a testament to the transformative power of these principles. I hope that by sharing this journey and the lessons learned along the way, I can help others unlock the potential of compassion, creativity, and connection in their own lives.

I've come to embrace change as a catalyst for growth, particularly when addressing the deep-seated issues of racism and social justice in

America. These are not topics one can shy away from. They demand our attention, our courage, and our unwavering commitment to seeking justice. I yearned to do more, to be more, in the face of these challenges.

In 2020, during the global pandemic and after the tragic murder of George Floyd, I gave birth to the *Bill Myers Inspires* podcast. It was created to facilitate hard conversations about racism and social justice, where uncomfortable topics are not avoided but embraced, and where experts share insights. The podcast's mission is to bring forth a clearer understanding of the nuanced injustices that plague our society.

But more than that, it seeks to stir compassion, ignite creativity, and, most importantly, foster connections that transcend our divisions and perceived differences. These principles are what I have observed and experienced that have now become part of my daily practice.

By embracing the 3 C's, we heal, we build, and we strengthen our understanding of how we are all interconnected as one race with a shared humanity. Doing this helps us unlock the potential for true happiness, peace, and justice.

Through my journey, I've understood that this is the only path that promises a brighter future for us all. And it is this path that I hope to guide others to walk down, one step at a time, one story at a time.

Decoding the 3 C's: Your Life's Secret Sauce

The 3 C's - Compassion, Creativity, and Connection - form the cornerstone of a fulfilling life and unlock our full potential as human beings.

Compassion, the heartbeat of our shared humanity, extends beyond helping others to enhancing our own emotional well-being. It's about recognizing suffering and taking action to alleviate it, both in ourselves and others.

Creativity transcends artistic pursuits, encompassing innovative problem-solving and seeing possibilities where others see dead-ends. It's our ability to generate novel ideas and solutions, contributing to personal growth and societal progress.

Connection, the invisible thread binding us together, provides a sense of belonging crucial for our well-being. It's about building and nurturing relationships that support us through life's challenges and amplify its joys.

These three elements intertwine, each reinforcing the others. Recent scientific research has demonstrated the profound impact of cultivating these qualities on our mental, emotional, and physical well-being. Now that we've explored each of the 3 C's individually, let's see how they work together to create profound change in real-life situations The following example illustrates the link between compassion, creativity, and connection.

3 C's: Catalysts for Change

Let's look at how these three powerful forces work together in real life. Consider Sarah, a young entrepreneur with a passion for the environment. She had always dreamed of making a difference but wasn't sure how.

One day, while walking on a beach littered with plastic waste, she felt a deep pang of compassion for the marine life affected by pollution. This compassion lit a spark of creativity in her. *"What if I could create products that replace single-use plastics?"* she thought, her eyes brightening with possibility.

Energized by this idea, Sarah began reaching out and connecting with like-minded individuals, from materials scientists with innovative ideas, to local community leaders with grassroots knowledge. Together, they brainstormed and developed eco-friendly alternatives to common plastic items.

Sarah's journey shows us the magic that happens when the 3 C's "dance" together -- compassion fueling creativity, and both leading to meaningful connections. Her story isn't just about personal transformation; it's about creating ripples of change that could help heal our oceans.

> *Compassion, creativity, and connection are powerful on their own, like individual instruments in an orchestra. But when combined, they create a symphony of positive change, an unstoppable force for growth and impact.*

By weaving them into the fabric of our daily lives, we not only enrich our own experiences, but we also contribute to designing a more beautiful world.

You might wonder why compassion, creativity, and connection are critical to our personal growth and fulfillment. Let's break this down. When we practice compassion, we permit ourselves to be human. We learn forgiveness and empathy, which makes us more understanding and less judgmental. When we take action to ease the suffering of others, this opens us up to deeper relationships and a more profound sense of peace within ourselves.

Creativity fuels our growth. It pushes us to step outside of our comfort zone, learn, and explore. The more we create, the more we discover about ourselves and the world around us. Creativity is a journey that continually challenges and rewards us with new insights and skills. As we grow more creative, we find fulfillment in our ability to express ourselves and contribute something unique to the world.

Then there's connection. Humans are social creatures. We thrive on relationships and community. By nurturing our connections with others, we build networks that help us grow. We learn from those around us, gain new experiences, and find joy in shared moments.

These connections can also drive social change. When we come together, united by common goals and values, we have the power to shift societies and make our voices heard. By focusing on these three pillars, we build a firm foundation for a life well-lived.

And it's not just about personal gain. These qualities are contagious. They spread outward, influencing others, reshaping communities, and even altering the course of history.

Embracing the 3 C's can lead to powerful transformations in our lives. By infusing our lives with these qualities, we become better individuals and contribute to a more vibrant, compassionate, and creative world.

It's a journey well worth taking. And it starts with a simple choice: to open our hearts and minds to the transformative power of compassion, creativity, and connection.

As we've seen, the 3 C's have the power to revolutionize our lives and the world around us. But how do we begin this transformative journey? Let's explore a practical roadmap for incorporating compassion, creativity, and connection into our daily lives.

Understanding the 3 C's

Let's dive right in. There is a journey ahead. Every step along this journey focuses on nurturing our compassion, creativity, and connection with others. Each step is a part of a larger path. This path is not just about reading. It's about doing. It's about changing how we live each day.

Here's the thing. We all want to feel good. We want to be happy. But happiness isn't just about what we have. It's about what we do. It's about how we treat others. It's about what we create. It's about how we connect. Sharing my journey will show you how to build a life that feels good on the inside, not just one that looks good on the outside.

Every step of the way, I'll be with you. And using my life experiences, I'll show you how connection is the glue. It's what holds us together with other people. It's what makes life rich and full.

What's the end goal? It's about transformation. This book is designed to help you become the best version of yourself as you find a deep sense of purpose. It's about living a life full of love, laughter, and learning. And the best part? This kind of life is not just for us. It makes the world a better place, too.

So, are you prepared to take these steps? Are you ready to learn, grow, and change? Are you ready to build a life about more than just getting by? A life that's about thriving, caring, and creating? If you are, then let's get going. This is your roadmap. It's time to start the journey to personal growth and fulfillment. We'll start with how the 3 C's can be powerful tools in navigating and shaping social change.

Navigating Social Change

Let's talk about change. Big change! The kind of change that shakes the ground and moves mountains. But let's keep it simple and clear, like how friends chat over coffee. I told you earlier that I started the *Bill Myers Inspires* podcast. It wasn't just a hobby. It was a mission -- a way to speak up about the wrongs in the world, especially racism and social justice issues that plague America. Serious stuff! It's about being fair and right with everyone, regardless of skin color or origin.

You see, we all share this world, and it's not just a place we live. It's a place we shape with our actions and our words. That's where the 3 C's come in. We all want to live in a world that's fair and kind. To make it happen, we must see each other as people not too different from us.

We all have hopes and dreams, with the same need to be loved and respected. To do this, we must open our eyes. We must listen. And we must speak out against what is unjust. That's being compassionate. That's being creative in finding solutions. And that's connecting with others to make a better world.

But why are these 3 C's so important for social change? Well, think about it. When you care for someone, you don't want to see them hurt. You want to help them. That's compassion. When you think outside the box, you can devise ways to fix things that aren't working. That's creativity. And when you reach out and work with others, you're not alone. You're a team. That's a connection. Together, these 3 C's do amazing things.

Take the podcast, for instance, where it's not just me talking. It's the guests sharing their expertise and stories. The listeners giving their questions and feedback. A bunch of voices are coming together to talk about hard things. And guess what? It's working. People are listening. They're talking. They're changing their minds and hearts. And bit by bit, they're changing the world.

Now, this isn't just about getting along. It's about doing what's right and making sure everyone gets a fair shake in life. Fairness. Equity. These are big words, too. But they just mean that everyone should be treated the same.

So, how do you fit into all this? You're not too small to make a difference. No way. Every voice counts. Every action matters. When you show compassion, you're saying, *"I care."* When you get creative, you say, "I've got ideas." And when you connect, you say, "Let's do this together." It's powerful. It's how we move forward. It's how we make the world better for all of us.

Think of it this way. If you saw someone fall, you'd help them up, right? That's compassion. If you devised a way to stop people from falling in the first place, that's creativity. And if you convinced others to help you, that's connection.

It's just like that with social change. We see the problems. We find ways to fix them. And we work with others to make it happen.

This is your call to action, to join in, to be part of something bigger than yourself. Use your heart, mind, and hands to build a world where everyone feels like they belong, where everyone is safe, where everyone can be happy. It starts with you, right here, right now.

And don't think you have to do big things to make a change. Small steps count. Start by listening to someone whose appearance and opinions are different from you. Try to understand their story. Share yours. Be kind. Think of new ways to help. Get your friends and family to join you. Every little bit adds to the big picture.

Remember, this isn't something you just read and forget. It is something to do, to live, to be. It's about using the 3 C's to touch lives and shape the world. It's about being brave and bold. It's about not giving up, even when it's hard, because together, we can make things right.

So, let's start today. Let's be the change we want to see. Let's inspire others to join us. Let's make our shared home a place where justice, fairness, and love aren't just words. They're real. They're here. They're us. As we embark on this journey of personal transformation, let's begin by looking inward and developing a deeper understanding of ourselves.

REFLECTIONS - CHAPTER 1: THE 3 C's REVOLUTION

Personal Assessment Questions:

1. How do you currently express compassion in your daily life?
2. Where do you see opportunities to be more creative in solving problems?
3. What meaningful connections have you made recently?
4. How do these 3 C's currently show up in your work and relationships?
5. Which of the 3 C's feels most natural to you, and which needs more development?

Weekly 3 C's Tracker:

1. **Compassion Monitor** □ Count daily acts of kindness □ Note emotional responses □ Track opportunities for compassion □ Record impact on others
2. **Creativity Compass** □ Document new ideas or solutions □ Note creative approaches to challenges □ Track moments of innovative thinking □ Record inspiration sources
3. **Connection Counter** □ Tally meaningful conversations □ Note depth of interactions □ Track new connections made □ Record strengthened relationships

Implementation Tips:

- Start with small, manageable actions
- Choose one C to focus on each day
- Document both successes and challenges
- Notice how the 3 C's interact

REFLECTIONS - Chapter 1: The 3 C's Revolution

Your 3 C's Journey Begins

As you embark on this transformative journey with the 3 C's, take a moment to reflect on where you are starting from and where you hope to go. This is your space to explore thoughts, feelings, and aspirations about integrating compassion, creativity, and connection into your life.

Journal Prompts:

- Describe a recent experience where you saw the 3 C's in action
- What excites you most about this journey?
- Which aspect of the 3 C's feels most challenging?
- How do you envision your life changing as you develop these qualities?

Space for Personal Notes:

Weekly Intention Setting: Choose one small action for each C to practice this week:

Compassion: _____

Creativity: _____

Connection: _____

Remember: This journey begins with awareness. Start by noticing opportunities for the 3 C's in your daily life. Each small step builds momentum toward meaningful transformation.

What stands out from Chapter 1 that you want to remember and implement?

COMING ATTRACTIONS

THE JOURNEY WITHIN

begins with a single step into...

NEXT QUEST!

UNVEILING
YOUR AUTHENTIC
SELF

"A quest that will change everything..."

VENTURE INTO THE DEPTHS OF:

HIDDEN PASSIONS

"Discover treasures within yourself!"

UNTOLD POTENTIAL

"Unlock your greatest gifts!"

TRUE DESTINY

"The revelation awaits..."

CHAPTER 2

THE QUEST BEGINS!

2

UNVEILING YOUR AUTHENTIC SELF

"Knowing yourself is the beginning of all wisdom."
— Aristotle

Self-awareness sits at the heart of personal growth, encompassing a deep understanding of your emotions, thoughts, behaviors, core values, and passions. It's an exploratory journey into your inner landscape, uncovering what drives and guides you.

Have you ever wondered what's really going on in your brain when you're being self-aware? It's pretty fascinating stuff! Dr. Tasha Eurich, an Organizational Psychologist and researcher, has done groundbreaking work in this field. She defines self-awareness as *"the ability to see ourselves clearly — to understand who we are, how others see us, and how we fit into the world."*

Here's where it gets really interesting. Dr. Eurich's research shows a significant gap between perceived and actual self-awareness. While 95% of people think they're self-aware, only about 10-15% actually are. This gap highlights why we need to actively work on developing this crucial skill.

Dr. Eurich tells us that there are two types of self-awareness: internal (how we see ourselves) and external (understanding how others view us). Your brain has specific areas that work together to make this happen, like a well-coordinated team effort in your head!

Think of self-awareness as a potent tool. When you have it, you can see what makes you happy, sad, and everything in between. This knowledge helps you make better decisions and align your actions with your true self. It's like being your own boss, but with a clearer understanding of the employee (you!).

Self-awareness is also closely linked to emotional intelligence, a concept popularized by Dr. Daniel Goleman. He emphasizes that self-awareness is the cornerstone of emotional intelligence, stating, *"If you can't recognize your own emotions, you'll have a tough time managing them or spotting them in others."* By working on your self-awareness, you're boosting your overall emotional smarts!

But it doesn't stop at emotions. Self-awareness helps you understand your thoughts and how they shape your life. When you're aware of your thought patterns, you can challenge and change the ones that don't serve you. For instance, if you catch yourself thinking, *"I can't do this,"* you can reframe it to *"I can learn to do this."*

As we deepen our self-awareness, a crucial step is to identify our personal passions and core values. Let's explore how to uncover these essential aspects of ourselves.

Core Values Discovery

Your core values are like a compass guiding your life's journey. They're the things you hold dear, the beliefs that light up your path. Think about this: when you make choices that match your values, you feel good inside. It's like everything clicks into place.

Dr. Brené Brown, renowned for her work on vulnerability and courage, emphasizes the importance of knowing our values. She says, *"Living into our values means that we do more than profess our values, we practice them. We walk our talk—we are clear about what we believe and hold important, and we take care that our intentions, words, thoughts, and behaviors align with those beliefs."*

So, how do we find these values? It's like going on a treasure hunt inside yourself. For example, you might realize that many of your proudest moments involved helping others. This could show that compassion or service is one of your core values. Or you might notice that your happiest memories involve creating something new, suggesting that creativity is a core value for you.

Understanding your core values is crucial because they influence every decision you make, often without you even realizing it. When you live in alignment with your values, you feel more fulfilled and authentic. As Dr. Brown suggests, it's not just about knowing your values, but also about practicing them consistently in your daily life.

Remember, this isn't about finding the "right" values. It's about discovering what truly matters to you. Your values are as unique as you are, and they're a big part of what makes you -- well, YOU!

So, take your time with this. Explore your memories, listen to your heart, and be honest with yourself. You might be surprised by what you discover! And once you've identified your values, challenge yourself to live them out, just as Dr. Brown encourages. It's in this alignment of beliefs and actions that we find our truest selves.

Sometimes, discovering our core values can lead to profound changes in our lives. Consider the story of Lisa, a successful corporate lawyer who always felt something was missing in her life.

Through a process of self-discovery, she realized that one of her core values was environmental conservation. This realization led her to transition her career to environmental law, where she found a deep sense of purpose and fulfillment.

Lisa's story shows us how powerful it can be when we identify and honor our core values. But you don't need to make a dramatic career change to live your values because small, everyday choices can make a big difference too.

Let's play a little game to uncover your core values. Grab a pen and paper and give yourself about fifteen minutes. Ready? Here we go:

- Think about a time when you felt really proud. What was happening?
- When have you felt most fulfilled? What were you doing?
- What would you stand up for, no matter what?
- If you could fight for one cause, what would it be?

Now, look at your answers. Do you see any patterns or recurring themes? They're probably your core values. Pretty cool how they show up, isn't it?

Here's a question to ponder: How do these values show up in your everyday life? For example, if "integrity" is one of your core values, how does it affect your choices at work or with friends?

Oh, and here's something to watch out for — sometimes, our values might clash with each other. Ever felt torn between "adventure" and "security?" It happens! When it does, think about the specific situation and your big-picture goals. Which value feels more important right now?

Emotional Intelligence Bootcamp

Emotions are signposts on your journey of self-discovery. They provide valuable information about what matters to you and how you relate to the world. Developing emotional intelligence is key to self-awareness.

Dr. Marc Brackett, Founding Director of the Yale Center for Emotional Intelligence, emphasizes the importance of emotional literacy. In his book *Permission to Feel*, he introduces the "RULER" approach: Recognizing, Understanding, Labeling, Expressing, and Regulating emotions.

Start by simply noticing your emotions throughout the day. What makes you feel joy? What triggers frustration? Don't judge these emotions; just observe them. Over time, you'll discover patterns that can offer profound insights into your inner world.

For instance, you might notice that you feel energized and excited when working on creative projects but drained and irritable after long meetings. This information can help you make choices that align with your emotional needs and preferences.

Now that we're getting to know our emotions better, let's talk about some cool tricks to manage them. Think of these as your emotional superpowers!

The Body Scan: Ever tried checking in with your body from head to toe? It's like giving yourself a quick emotional health check!

Name It to Tame It: This one's fun. Next time you're feeling a strong emotion, try to name it. It's like calling out the monster under the bed and suddenly it's not so scary anymore!

The 90-Second Rule: Did you know that the physical rush of an emotion typically only lasts about 90 seconds? Next time you're feeling overwhelmed, try to breathe through it. Can you feel it pass?

Which of these do you think you'll try first? Imagine how much easier decision-making and hanging out with friends could be if you had better control over your emotions!

Passion Compass

> *What lights you up? What activities make you lose track of time? These are clues to your passions. Identifying and nurturing your interests is a crucial part of self-discovery.*

Dr. Angela Duckworth, known for her research on grit, suggests that passion often develops over time through exploration and deepening engagement. She encourages people to try many different activities and pay attention to what captures their interest.

Think back to when you were a child. What did you love to do? Sometimes, our truest passions are those we've carried with us since childhood. Or consider what topics you find yourself constantly reading about or discussing with others. These might be areas of passion you haven't fully explored yet.

Take the example of John, who always enjoyed tinkering with computers as a hobby. As he explored this interest more deeply, he discovered a passion for coding, and eventually he transitioned from his job in sales to a fulfilling career as a software developer.

Have you ever been so wrapped up in doing something you love that you lost track of time? That's what psychologists call "flow." Cool word, right? It's like you're in a bubble where everything just clicks.

Want to get into this flow state more often? Here are some tips:

- Pick activities that challenge you more than what you're used to.
- Set clear goals. What are you aiming for?
- Look for quick feedback. How will you know you're on the right track?
- Cut out distractions. What tends to pull your attention away?

Think about the last time you experienced flow. What were you doing? That might be a big clue about what really lights you up inside!

Strengths Spotlight

Everyone has unique strengths and areas for growth. Recognizing these helps you leverage your talents and identify opportunities for personal development. Dr. Martin Seligman, a pioneer in Positive

Psychology, developed the *"VIA Character Strengths Survey,"* a tool to help people identify their core strengths. He argues that using our strengths regularly leads to greater well-being and life satisfaction.

Ask yourself what comes naturally to you and what others often compliment you on. These might be your strengths. Similarly, ask what you find challenging or in what area(s) you often struggle. These could be areas for growth.

Remember, the goal isn't to be perfect at everything, but to understand yourself better so you can make choices that play to your strengths, while also challenging you to grow.

Reflection: The Self-Discovery Tool

Regular reflection is a powerful tool for self-awareness. It allows you to process experiences, learn from them, and gain deeper insights into yourself. Dr. Jennifer Porter, an executive and team coach, emphasizes the importance of reflection in her *Harvard Business Review* article. She states, *"Reflection gives the brain an opportunity to pause amidst the chaos, untangle and sort through observations and experiences, consider multiple possible interpretations, and create meaning."*

Try setting aside a few minutes each day for reflection. You might write in a journal, meditate, or simply sit quietly and think about your day. Consider responding to these questions: *"What did I learn today? How did I feel? What am I grateful for?"*

Ready to supercharge your self-awareness? Let's try this reflection practice for one week. It's like giving your brain a chance to process everything that's happened.

Victories: What were 2-3 things you totally "nailed" this week?

Tough Stuff: What were two tricky situations you faced? How did you handle them?

"Aha" Moments: Write down 1-2 new things you learned about yourself. Any surprises?

Gratitude Check: What are 1-2 things you're thankful for right now?

Coming Up: Based on all this, what are two goals you want to set for next week?

How does it feel to look back on your week like this? Pretty eye-opening, right?

Feedback: Your Growth Catalyst

While self-reflection is important, gaining insights from others can provide valuable perspectives on your blind spots and hidden strengths. Dr. David Dunning, known for his work on the *Dunning-Kruger Effect*, emphasizes the importance of seeking external feedback. He argues that we often have blind spots in assessing our own abilities, and that input from others can provide crucial insights.

Don't be afraid to ask trusted friends or mentors for their honest feedback. You might ask, *"What do you see as my strengths?"* or *"Where do you think I have room to grow?"* Their answers might offer new avenues for your self-discovery.

Embracing Change: The Growth Mindset

Self-discovery is an ongoing process. As you grow and change, so do your values and understanding of yourself. Embrace this evolution as a natural part of your journey.

Dr. Carol Dweck, Psychologist and Professor at *Stanford University*, has conducted groundbreaking research on the concept of "mindset." Her work, which has revolutionized our understanding of success and achievement, introduces the idea of a "growth mindset."

Dweck's studies, published in her influential book, *Mindset: The New Psychology of Success*, suggest that viewing our abilities and personalities as capable of development rather than fixed leads to greater success and fulfillment.

This perspective encourages individuals to embrace challenges, persist in the face of setbacks, and view effort as a path to mastery. Remember, the person you are today is not the same person you were five years ago, and that's a good thing. Growth and change are signs that you're learning and evolving.

Let's talk about how knowing yourself better can seriously level up your relationships. Have you ever thought about how your self-awareness impacts the way you interact with others? Here's something to "chew on." Your attachment style is like your relationship personality. Are you secure, anxious, avoidant, or a mix? Knowing this can be a game-changer in understanding your relationship patterns.

Want to boost your relationship self-awareness? Try this: In your next chat with someone, pay attention to the emotions that come up for you. Notice whether your body is leaning in or pulling back. You'll be able to discern how well you are listening by taking notice of whether you're quick to judge or patiently understanding. After that interaction, take a minute to think about any patterns you discover about yourself.

Remember, getting to know yourself better isn't just fun -- it's the key to living a life that truly feels like "you." Your journey of self-discovery is just beginning, and I can't wait to see where it takes you!

Self-Discovery In Action

As part of your practice to keep a journal, you might create a personal mission statement based on your core values. You could also take a personality assessment like the *Big Five* or Myers-Briggs Type Indicator for additional insights.

As you continue on this journey of self-discovery, remember that the goal is not perfection, but authenticity. By understanding your values, emotions, and unique qualities, you're laying the foundation for a life aligned with your true self. This self-awareness will guide you in making choices that resonate with who you are at your core.

Self-awareness is like learning to read; once you know how, a whole new world opens up to you. It's the key to personal growth, better relationships, and a more fulfilling life. So, take the step to work on your self-awareness and watch as your life improves, step by step, day by day.

As Dr. Eurich says, *"Self-awareness isn't one truth. It's a delicate balance of two distinct, even competing, viewpoints."* It's about understanding both your internal perspective and how others see you. This comprehensive view of yourself is what will truly empower you to live authentically and make meaningful changes in your life.

Breaking Self-Awareness Barriers

While the journey of self-discovery is rewarding, it's not always easy. We often encounter internal barriers that hinder our progress. Dr. Tasha Eurich identifies several "invisible roadblocks" to self-awareness in her research:

The Cult of Self: Our self-absorbed culture can make it challenging to view ourselves objectively.

The Confirmation Bias: We tend to seek information that confirms our existing beliefs about ourselves.

The Instant Gratification Loop: The quick hits of validation we get from social media can distract us from deeper self-reflection.

To overcome these barriers, Dr. Eurich suggests practices like mindfulness meditation, seeking out candid feedback, and regularly challenging our assumptions about ourselves.

Relationships as Mirrors

Our relationships play a crucial role in our journey of self-discovery. Dr. Susan David, *Harvard Medical School* Psychologist, emphasizes the importance of "emotional agility" in relationships. She argues that our interactions with others can provide valuable insights into our own patterns of thought and behavior.

Consider the story of Thomas, who always thought of himself as a patient person. However, through feedback from his partner and close friends, he realized that he often became irritable when things didn't go according to plan. This insight led Thomas to work on his flexibility and stress management, ultimately improving both his self-awareness and his relationships.

Self-Compassion: Your Inner Ally

As we embark on this journey of self-discovery, it's crucial to approach ourselves with kindness and compassion. Dr. Kristin Neff, a pioneer in **S**elf-compassion research, defines self-compassion as having three components:

- Self-kindness vs. Self-judgment
- Common humanity vs. Isolation
- Mindfulness vs. Over-identification

Dr. Neff's research shows that individuals who practice self-compassion are more likely to have the courage to look at themselves honestly and make necessary changes. They're also more resilient in the face of challenges and setbacks.

Try this self-compassion exercise:

The next time you face a difficulty or mistake, imagine how you would speak to a dear friend in the same situation. Then, try to offer yourself the same kindness and understanding.

Culture Lenses on Self-Awareness

Our cultural background significantly influences how we perceive ourselves and the world around us. Dr. Hazel Rose Markus, Social Psychologist at Stanford University, has extensively researched how culture shapes the self.

For instance, in many Western cultures, there's a strong emphasis on individuality and personal achievement. In contrast, many Eastern cultures prioritize harmony and interconnectedness. Understanding these cultural influences can provide a valuable context for our self-discovery journey.

For example, Aisha, who grew up in a collectivist culture but now lives in an individualistic society, found herself struggling with career decisions. Through self-reflection, she realized she needed to balance her cultural value of family responsibility with her personal aspirations. This awareness helped her make choices that honored both aspects of her identity.

Living Self-Aware: Daily Practices

The ultimate goal of self-awareness is to understand ourselves better, and also to use that understanding to live more fulfilling lives. Here are some practical ways to integrate self-awareness into your daily routine:

Morning Intention Setting: Start each day by setting an intention based on your core values.

Mindful Breaks: Take short breaks throughout the day to check in with your thoughts and emotions.

Evening Reflection: End each day with a brief reflection on how your actions aligned with your values and goals.

Weekly Reflection: At the end of a week, consider the power of the interaction between intentions and reflections.

Dr. Laurie Santos, Psychology Professor at *Yale University* created a course on happiness that emphasizes the importance of making these practices habitual. She suggests starting small and being consistent, allowing these self-awareness practices to become a natural part of your daily life.

REFLECTIONS - CHAPTER 2: UNVEILING YOUR AUTHENTIC SELF

Self-Discovery Assessment:

1. What activities make you lose track of time?
2. When do you feel most energized and alive?
3. How do you usually process feedback from others?
4. What values guide your important decisions?
5. Where do you feel most authentically yourself?

Weekly Authenticity Tracker:

1. **Core Values Monitor** ▫ Record decisions made today ▫ Note alignment with values ▫ Track moments of internal conflict ▫ Document value-based choices
2. **Self-Awareness Practice** ▫ Morning intention setting ▫ Evening reflection ▫ Emotional awareness checks ▫ Body-mind connection moments
3. **Authentic Expression** ▫ Times you spoke your truth ▫ Moments of vulnerability ▫ Authentic interactions ▫ Self-censoring instances

Implementation Tips:

- Practice daily self-reflection
- Notice when you feel most/least authentic
- Track energy levels in different situations
- Document what supports/hinders authenticity

REFLECTIONS - CHAPTER 2: UNVEILING YOUR AUTHENTIC SELF

Your Authentic Journey

Self-discovery is an ongoing journey of uncovering who you truly are beneath social expectations and learned behaviors. Use this space to explore your authentic self with curiosity and compassion.

Journal Prompts:

- What masks do you wear in different situations?
- When do you feel most free to be yourself?
- What parts of yourself do you wish to express more fully?
- Who helps you feel safe to be authentic?

Deep Dive Questions:

- What childhood dreams still resonate?
- Which compliments feel truly meaningful?
- What do you want to be remembered for?

Space for Personal Insights:

Weekly Intention: Choose one way to express your authentic self this week:

Remember: Authenticity develops through gentle exploration and honest reflection. Be patient with yourself as you uncover and embrace your true nature.

What new insights about yourself emerged from Chapter 2?

COMING ATTRACTIONS

THE CHART-TOPPING SELF-HELP HIT

NOW DROPPING!

THE SCIENCE OF COMPASSION

FEATURING THE HITS:

1. Journey to the Brain's Compassion Center (Extended Mix)
2. Empathy Remix (feat. Leading Neuroscientists)
3. Symphony of Positive Change (Club Mix)
4. Ripples of Kindness (Community Remix)

PRODUCED BY THE CREATORS OF
"Unveiling Your Authentic Self"

AVAILABLE IN CHAPTER 3 ★ LIMITED ENGAGEMENT

3
———————

THE SCIENCE OF COMPASSION

"What lies behind us and what lies before us are tiny matters
compared to what lies within us."
— Ralph Waldo Emerson

Why Compassion Matters

Compassion is a word we often hear, but what does it really mean? Compassion goes beyond kindness or sympathy. It's recognizing others' suffering and choosing to alleviate it—a powerful force driving us to actively help, not just empathize.

Imagine a world where everyone acknowledges and alleviates each other's pain. This transformative power of compassion is like a warm hug for the soul, benefiting both giver and receiver.

As the heartbeat of our shared humanity, compassion compels us to help someone who's fallen, or to listen deeply to a troubled friend, or to volunteer for those in need. It's not just making the world kinder—it's transforming it, one act at a time.

Excitingly, science reveals that compassion benefits us too. When we feel and act on genuine compassion, our brain lights up like a Christmas tree, particularly in emotion-handling areas. Caring for others literally makes our brains happier and healthier.

Dr. Richard Davidson, a renowned Neuroscientist, has shown that compassion meditation activates brain regions linked to positive emotions and empathy. His research reveals that practicing compassion enhances our own emotional well-being while we are helping others.

When we empathize and act to help, our brain releases feel-good chemicals—the same ones triggered by a hug. This can reduce our stress levels, as if our brain is patting us on the back for caring and then acting. Thus, addressing others' suffering becomes a form of self-care, often leaving us feeling great after helping someone.

> *Compassion transcends empathy, compelling us to actively ease suffering. As we practice it, we're rewiring our brains.*

Neuroscience reveals that compassionate acts activate brain regions associated with positive emotions and reward, creating a positive feedback loop of wellbeing that benefits both giver and receiver—a beautiful illustration of our shared human experience.

The benefits of compassion extend beyond momentary feel-good sensations. Long-term health perks include a bolstered immune system. Imagine giving your body both a shield and a sword against germs. It can also slow your heart rate, offering your hardworking hearts a welcome breather.

Mentally, compassion equips us with tools to better handle our own challenges. It fosters stronger social connections too, because when we're actively supportive, people naturally gravitate towards us. These friendships, in turn, combat loneliness and boost overall happiness.

As we look into the neuroscience of compassion in the following sections, we'll discover even more fascinating ways that this powerful force shapes our brains and our lives. Get ready to explore the incredible science behind what happens in our brains when we choose to care and act compassionately!

Compassion's Neural Footprint

Let's delve deeper into the neuroscience of compassion. Don't worry if you're not a science whiz. I'll break it all down for you. Neuroscientist and Psychologist, Dr. Tania Singer, has pioneered studies on the neural basis of empathy and compassion.

In a landmark study published in Social Cognitive and Affective Neuroscience, Dr. Singer's team used fMRI (functional Magnetic Resonance Imaging) to observe brain activity during compassion meditation.

Their findings were remarkable! Compassion meditation increased activity in several key brain regions:

- Medial Orbitofrontal Cortex and Ventral Striatum: Associated with positive emotions and rewards.
- Anterior Insula and Anterior Cingulate Cortex: Linked to empathy and understanding others' emotions.

Temporoparietal Junction: Crucial for perspective-taking and understanding others' mental states."

These brain changes often coincide with the release of oxytocin—the "love hormone" or "cuddle chemical"—produced in the hypothalamus and released by the pituitary gland. Critical for the process of social bonding, empathy, and trust, oxytocin is released during compassionate acts or thoughts, enhancing our feelings of connection and care.

While our past doesn't dictate our future, it profoundly shapes our connections. Reflecting on my own pivotal moments, let me share more of my grandfather's and father's wisdom that helped to shape my childhood experiences.

My grandfather's lesson on borrowing money illustrated how compassion and clear communication strengthen bonds, even in challenging situations. My father's "Officer Friendly" presentations showed how creative thinking can bridge community gaps, highlighting the fact that building authentic relationships require stepping out of our comfort zones. Finally, my hearing Louis Armstrong play revealed how shared passions create instant, meaningful connections.

These experiences demonstrate that authentic relationships are built on compassion, nurtured through creative understanding, and deepened by resonant shared moments. As you reflect on your journey, remember that your personal insights, while invaluable, are just the beginning.

Recent scientific research has unveiled fascinating physiological aspects of human bonding, leading us to an exciting frontier: the study of heart-brain coherence. By integrating our lived experiences with these scientific insights, we can develop a richer understanding of nurturing authentic relationships.

Dr. Singer's research goes beyond observing initial changes. In a longitudinal study spanning several months, her team investigated how different types of mental training affect brain plasticity.

Participants undergoing compassion training showed lasting changes in brain regions associated with social cognition and emotional regulation. Specifically, they observed increased gray matter volume in the right anterior insula and right inferior parietal lobule, which are areas that are important for developing empathy and compassion.

This research robustly demonstrates that compassion isn't a fixed trait, but a skill that can be cultivated and strengthened over time. It leads to measurable changes in brain structure and function, as well as increased production of oxytocin in the body.

As we explore the neuroscience of compassion, we see how it forms the foundation for the other C's. A compassionate brain is more open to creative solutions and more adept at forming meaningful connections.

Empathy in Action

Let's explore the neuroscience of empathy, which is closely related to compassion. Dr. Helen Riess, Associate Professor of Psychiatry at *Harvard Medical School*, has illuminated the neurobiological basis of empathy in her research published in the *Journal of Continuing Education in the Health Professions.*

Dr. Riess explains that empathy involves multiple brain regions working in concert. The Mirror Neuron System helps us understand others' actions and intentions. The Limbic System allows resonance with others' feelings. And the Prefrontal Cortex regulates emotions and makes reasoned decisions based on empathic understanding.

Empathy is closely tied to oxytocin. When we empathize, our brains often release oxytocin, enhancing our ability to understand and share others' feelings. This creates a positive feedback loop: empathy triggers oxytocin release, which further increases our capacity for empathy.

Building on these insights, Dr. Riess developed an empathy training program incorporating mindfulness and emotional recognition techniques. This program significantly increased participants' empathy scores and improved their ability to accurately read others' emotions.

A randomized controlled trial published in the Journal of General Internal Medicine showed that doctors who underwent this training demonstrated significant improvements in patient-rated empathy scores, as compared to a control group. While not directly measured, increased oxytocin production likely played a role in these improvements, given its known effects on empathy and social bonding.

This research underscores that empathy, like compassion, has a neurobiological basis that can be strengthened through targeted training. The intricate interplay between brain activity, structural changes, and hormone production (particularly oxytocin) highlights the complex nature of our capacity for empathy and compassion.

By understanding these biological mechanisms, we can better appreciate how practices like meditation, acts of kindness, and empathy training can literally change our brains and bodies, making us more attuned to the feelings of others and more inclined toward compassionate action.

Global Compassion Perspectives

Understanding these biological mechanisms helps us appreciate how practices like meditation, acts of kindness, and empathy training can physically alter our brains and bodies. These changes make us more attuned to others' feelings and inclined towards compassionate action.

Compassion isn't confined to Western thought—it's celebrated globally. One beautiful example comes from Africa, with a philosophy called Ubuntu meaning "I am because we are." This profound concept emphasizes our interconnectedness, suggesting that individual well-being is inextricably linked to collective welfare. Imagine basing every decision on its impact not just on you, but on everyone around you. That's Ubuntu in action—compassion elevated to a new level.

This idea of interconnectedness aligns perfectly with neuroscientific findings on compassion. When we internalize our collective interdependence, our brains are more likely to respond with kindness and understanding. It's as if Ubuntu and neuroscience are in harmony, both conveying the same message: compassion is the world's driving force.

Empathy & Understanding: The Compassion Bridge

When we interact with others, we crave understanding. This brings to mind one of my grandfather's core biblical mantra's: *"With all thy getting, get an understanding"* (Proverbs 4:7). You see, we share our stories, hoping others will grasp their meanings. This is the essence of empathy—understanding how someone else feels. May I ask you to recall a time of intense emotion where you likely wanted others to understand why you felt the way you did? This universal need for empathy underscores its importance in human connection.

Dr. Tania Singer's groundbreaking work, which we explored earlier, extends beyond compassion to empathy. As a leading expert, she's demonstrated that both compassion and empathy are not fixed traits, but skills we can cultivate.

Her studies show that regular mental training can enhance our capacity for empathy and compassion, leading to improved social connections and overall well-being. It's akin to exercising our emotional intelligence, which is a workout for our empathic abilities!

Empathy enhances our friendships and social interactions. Understanding others' feelings allows us to respond appropriately, offering comfort in sadness or sharing joy in happiness.

A key component of empathy is active listening—giving someone your full attention without planning your response. This practice, while challenging, deepens understanding. It's comparable to studying a picture; the longer you look, the more details you notice. Similarly, attentive listening reveals nuances in people's expressions and experiences.

Another vital aspect is suspending judgment. Instead of quickly categorizing someone's words or actions as right or wrong, we should strive to understand their perspective without immediate evaluation. This approach, which I know is really difficult, is essential for fostering genuine connections and being a supportive friend.

As your empathy grows, practicing compassion becomes more natural. To clarify the distinction: empathy is our ability to understand and share others' feelings, metaphorically putting ourselves in their shoes. Compassion takes this a step further—it's the desire to alleviate the suffering we've recognized through empathy, coupled with choosing to take a specific action.

In essence, empathy forms the foundation for compassionate acts. Without empathy's insight into others' pain, we lack the understanding necessary to be truly compassionate.

Loving-Kindness: A Mental Meditation

Let's explore a powerful tool for cultivating compassion -- loving-kindness meditation. Despite its fancy name, it's a simple, yet effective practice.

Dr. Barbara Fredrickson's exciting research on loving-kindness meditation reveals impressive results. This practice can boost positive emotions, enhance mindfulness, and improve overall life satisfaction. It's as if her work has unlocked new possibilities for nurturing compassion.

Ready to experience it? Here's a simple guide:

- Find a comfortable spot and close your eyes.
- Visualize someone you love, happy and smiling.
- Silently repeat: *"May you be happy. May you be healthy. May you be safe. May you live with ease."*
- Extend these wishes to yourself, a neutral person, someone you find difficult, and finally, all beings.

While it might feel awkward initially, persist. You're essentially giving your brain a compassion workout!

Kindness in Action

Now, let's put our compassion knowledge into action through acts of kindness. This practice not only benefits others, but also enhances your own well-being.

Dr. Sonja Lyubomirsky's research reveals that people who performed five acts of kindness weekly reported greater happiness than those who didn't. It's as if kindness is a boomerang—it returns to benefit the giver.

So, what counts as an act of kindness? It could be anything from helping a neighbor to carry groceries into the house, to sending a supportive text to a friend. The key is to offer genuine care without expectation of anything in return. It's about illuminating the world, one kind act at a time.

Compassion Stories: Real-World Impact

Compassion manifests in diverse and inspiring ways across cultures. Let's explore some compelling examples:

- Japan's *"moai"*: This practice involves small groups of people who meet regularly to provide emotional and financial support to one another. It's a lifelong commitment that integrates compassion directly into the social fabric, creating a safety net for its members.
- Sikh's *"langar"*: In Sikh temples (gurdwaras), free meals are served to anyone who comes, regardless of their religion, caste, gender, economic status, or ethnicity. This tradition embodies compassion through nourishment and emphasizes equality among all people.

- Indonesia's *"gotong royong"* (mutual assistance): This principle of communal work and support sees entire communities coming together to assist each other with various tasks. Whether building houses or planning weddings, it's a beautiful example of compassion scaled up to a community level.

These practices demonstrate how compassion can be seamlessly woven into daily life and community structures, offering powerful models for incorporating kindness into our own societies.

Overcoming Compassion Barriers

However, our innate biases and assumptions can sometimes hinder our ability to extend compassion universally. Dr. Jennifer Eberhardt, Social Psychologist, has conducted groundbreaking work on unconscious bias.

Her research reveals that while these biases are deeply ingrained in us, we can overcome them through conscious effort and consistent practice. It's akin to debugging our mental software, thus requiring patience and persistence.

Here's a practical challenge to expand your compassion: This week, make a conscious effort to notice when you're making quick judgments about others. When you catch yourself doing this, pause and ask, *"What else might be true about this person that I don't know?"*

This simple, yet powerful practice can help you extend compassion to individuals you might not typically connect with, thereby broadening your capacity for empathy and understanding.

Compassion Champions

Let's draw inspiration from real-life compassion superheroes:

- Jadav Payeng, the *"Forest Man of India,"* single-handedly planted a forest larger than Central Park over several decades. His profound compassion for the environment transformed a barren sandbar into a lush, 1,360-acre forest that became home to Bengal tigers, rhinoceros, and elephants. Payeng's dedication demonstrates how one person's compassionate action can restore an entire ecosystem.
- Francine Christophe, a Holocaust survivor, shared her last piece of chocolate with a pregnant woman in a concentration camp. Years later, at a conference where Christophe was speaking, a young psychologist revealed she was the baby born in the camp. She credited her mother's survival and her own birth to that small act of kindness, illustrating how compassion can echo through generations.
- Asep Kambali, known as the *"Pizza Man"* of Malang, Indonesia, has been distributing free pizza to those in need for years. What began as a way to use leftover ingredients has evolved into a mission that feeds hundreds weekly, showing how a simple act of kindness can grow into a sustained community initiative.

These stories underscore how seemingly small acts of compassion can profoundly impact individuals and communities.

On a global scale, figures like *Tenzin Gyatso*, the 14th Dalai Lama, embody compassion as a life principle. His teachings on kindness, empathy, and inner peace have inspired millions worldwide to embrace compassion as a daily, conscious choice rather than a mere feeling.

Closer to home, *Eckhart Tolle's* insights on mindfulness and present-moment awareness have touched countless lives. Tolle's work emphasizes cultivating compassion for us and others, which highlights our shared humanity and interconnectedness.

His teachings provide practical ways to integrate compassion into our daily lives, from our self-talk to our interactions with others.

These renowned figures demonstrate that compassion is a powerful guiding force, influencing personal actions and inspiring global movements. Their work illustrates compassion's ability to transcend cultural and geographical boundaries, creating a ripple effect of kindness that can transform individuals, communities, and potentially, the world.

Navigating Compassion Hurdles

Let's address a key truth: practicing compassion isn't always easy. It can be particularly challenging to extend kindness to those with whom we disagree, and those in caregiving professions may experience compassion fatigue—a state of physical and emotional exhaustion resulting from the constant demands of caring for others.

However, Dr. Kristin Neff, a pioneering researcher in self-compassion, offers a powerful solution. Her extensive studies show that being kind to ourselves is key to sustaining our capacity for compassion towards others.

It's akin to the airline safety instruction of putting on your own oxygen mask before assisting others. By nurturing self-compassion, we keep our "compassion tanks" full and ready to share with the world.

Dr. Neff's self-compassion is comprised of three core components:

- Self-kindness vs. Self-judgment
- Common humanity vs. Isolation
- Mindfulness vs. Over-identification

By cultivating these aspects, we can build resilience against compassion fatigue and enhance our overall well-being.

Ready to strengthen your "compassion muscles?" Here's an evidence-based exercise to track your progress:

Exercise: Compassion Counter

For one week, try to perform three kind acts each day, and keep a tally. Practice loving-kindness meditation for 5 minutes daily and rate your self-kindness each day on a scale of 1 to 10.

At week's end, review your scores. Pay attention, not just to the numbers, but also to how these practices have affected your mood, stress levels, and interactions with others. Many participants in similar studies reported significant increases in overall well-being and interpersonal connections.

This exercise, grounded in positive psychology research, can help you cultivate a more compassionate mindset. As you progress, you may notice an increased awareness of opportunities for kindness and a greater ease in extending compassion, both to yourself and others.

As we conclude our exploration of the neuroscience of compassion, let's reflect on the transformative journey we've undertaken. Remember, compassion isn't just a fleeting emotion, but a skill we can cultivate and strengthen. As the Dalai Lama wisely said, *"If you want others to be happy, practice compassion. If you want to be happy practice compassion."*

Throughout this chapter, we've delved into the fascinating world of compassion, uncovering its profound impact on our brains and lives. We've explored how this powerful force shapes our neural pathways, influences our well-being, and enhances our connections with others. This journey is about harnessing the power to create a more empathetic and connected world.

REFLECTIONS - Chapter 3: The Science of Compassion

Compassion Assessment:

1. How do you typically respond to others' suffering?
2. What triggers make compassion challenging?
3. How do you practice self-compassion?
4. When do you feel most/least compassionate?
5. How does compassion affect your wellbeing?

Weekly Compassion Tracker:

1. **Self-Compassion Monitor** ▫ Morning self-kindness practice ▫ Responses to personal mistakes ▫ Self-care moments ▫ Negative self-talk transformed
2. **Compassion for Others** ▫ Acts of kindness performed ▫ Empathy moments experienced ▫ Active listening practiced ▫ Support offered to others
3. **Compassion Impact** ▫ Changes in relationships ▫ Effects on personal stress ▫ Ripple effects observed ▫ Unexpected outcomes

Implementation Tips:

- Start with self-compassion
- Notice physical sensations of compassion
- Track mood before/after compassionate acts
- Document what supports/blocks compassion

REFLECTIONS - CHAPTER 3: THE SCIENCE OF COMPASSION

Your Compassion Journey

Understanding the science of compassion shows us how this powerful force can transform our brains and lives. Use this space to explore your growing capacity for compassion and its effects on you and others.

Journal Prompts:

- Describe a moment when compassion changed a situation
- How does your body feel when you're being compassionate?
- What helps you return to compassion when you're stressed?
- Who models compassion in your life?

Exploring Compassion:

- When did you first learn about compassion?
- What makes it easier/harder to be compassionate?
- How does compassion affect your relationships?

Space for Personal Insights:

Weekly Compassion Intention: Choose one way to deepen your compassion practice:

Remember: Compassion is a skill that strengthens with practice. Each compassionate act creates positive changes in your brain and ripples out to affect others.

What new understanding of compassion emerged from Chapter 3?

COMING ATTRACTIONS

EXCLUSIVE PREMIERE!

GET READY FOR THE
RELATIONSHIP EVENT
OF THE YEAR!

BUILDING
AUTHENTIC
CONNECTIONS

Starring a groundbreaking cast of

THE VULNERABILITY GROOVE

THE EMPATHY ECHO

THE TRUST-BUILDING BASSLINE

"Where chemistry sizzles both on and off camera!"

EVERY INTERACTION

is a red carpet event!

PREMIERING IN CHAPTER 4

4

BUILDING AUTHENTIC CONNECTIONS

*"Connection is why we're here; it is what gives
purpose and meaning to our lives."*
— Brené Brown

Have you ever felt that indescribable warmth when sharing a genuine laugh with a close friend, or enjoyed the comfort of knowing that someone truly understood you? These moments of authentic connection are the essential threads that weave together the rich tapestry of our lives.

In this chapter, we'll explore the foundations of authentic relationships, delving into what makes certain connections truly meaningful and how to cultivate them. We'll examine the qualities that breathe life into our interactions, embrace the transformative power of vulnerability, and further explore the African philosophy of Ubuntu, which we touched upon earlier.

Dr. John Gottman's work on relationship stability emphasizes that trust and commitment are foundational to strong relationships. *"Trust is built in very small moments,"* Gottman notes, which highlights the importance of everyday interactions in deepening our connections.

By the chapter's end, you'll have a toolkit for building and recognizing authentic relationships and understanding the power of empathetic communication to deepen your connections in profound ways.

In this chapter, we'll cover Understanding Qualities of Meaningful Relationships, Science of Heart-Brain Coherence, and Further Exploring of Ubuntu's Shared Humanity. All of this will lead us into The Power of Vulnerability, the Development of Empathetic Communication Skills, and the Integration of the 3 C's within Authentic Relationships

Are you ready to transform your relationships and your life? Let's discover the incredible power of authentic connections together.

Relationship Essentials

As we explore what makes relationships truly meaningful, I'm reminded of the profound lessons I've learned from my own life. My grandfather's compassionate approach to teaching me about financial responsibility, my father's creative way of connecting with the community through his "Officer Friendly" presentations, and the inspirational connection I felt listening to Louis Armstrong play were pivotal experiences that have shaped my understanding of authentic relationships.

We all yearn for connections that make us feel valued, don't we? Those are the relationships that stand strong through life's ups and downs. Let's explore together the qualities that breathe life into our most meaningful relationships.

Dr. John Gottman, a pioneer in understanding what makes relationships "tick," tells us that trust and commitment are the bedrock of strong connections. *"Trust is built in very small moments,"* he says. This reminds me of how my grandfather built up trust with me through his patient lessons. It's those everyday interactions that lay the foundation for something deeper.

Here are the key ingredients of meaningful relationships:

Trust and Commitment: The trust my grandfather fostered in me, it's the glue holding everything together.

Respect: The value placed upon each other's thoughts and feelings, even in disagreement. My father's approach to community policing exemplified his respect for diverse perspectives.

Support: The willingness to be there for each other through thick and thin. It's like the support I felt from my family as I pursued my passion for music, inspired by Louis Armstrong.

Communication: The ability to share our inner worlds with kindness and attentive listening. Good communication creates understanding, just as Armstrong's trumpet spoke volumes without words.

Loyalty: The desire to stand by each other, especially in tough times. It's the unwavering presence I've felt from my closest relationships.

Empathy: The determination to step into someone else's shoes, much like my father did in his community outreach. Dr. Brené Brown describes empathy as *"feeling with people."*

Growth: The belief that when we can grow together, our relationships become stronger and more resilient. Dr. Carol Dweck's ideas on growth mindset apply here.

To illustrate these principles in action, let's look at Sarah and Mike's story:

Case Study: Sarah and Mike's Journey to Empathy

Sarah and Mike, high school sweethearts married for ten years, found themselves drifting apart. Their once-vibrant connection had become strained by unmet expectations and miscommunications. Determined to rekindle their bond, they sought help from Dr. Lisa Chen, Relationship Therapist.

"When they first came to me," Dr. Chen recalls, *"they could barely have a conversation without it turning into an argument. Sarah felt unheard, while Mike felt constantly criticized."*

Dr. Chen introduced them to a series of empathy exercises designed to foster understanding and connection. One particularly effective exercise was the "Empathy Mirror." *"I asked them to practice 'feeling with' each other,"* Dr. Chen explained. *"Before responding to their partner's concern, they had to paraphrase what they heard and imagine how their partner might be feeling."*

For instance, when Sarah expressed frustration about Mike working late, instead of becoming defensive, Mike practiced the exercise, saying, *"It sounds like when I work late, you feel lonely and perhaps unimportant. Is that right?"* Sarah responded, *"Yes, that's exactly it. I miss our time together."* Mike said, *"I can understand how that would be frustrating. My intention isn't to make you feel that way."* This simple act of reflection and validation often diffused tensions before they could escalate.

Another powerful technique was the "Appreciation Jar." Each day, they wrote down one thing they appreciated about the other and placed it in a jar. At the end of each week, they read those notes together. *"This exercise helped them focus on the positive aspects of their relationship,"* Dr. Chen noted. *"It fostered gratitude and reminded them of why they fell in love in the first place."*

Within weeks, Sarah and Mike reported significant improvements. They were having fewer arguments, and when conflicts did arise, they were better equipped to handle them with empathy and understanding. *"The change in their body language was remarkable. They started sitting closer together, making eye contact, and even finishing each other's sentences again."*

This case illustrates how nurturing just empathy can transform a relationship. By learning to truly listen and understand each other, Sarah and Mike rebuilt their connection, making their bond stronger than ever.

As we reflect on Sarah and Mike's journey, consider how you might apply similar practices in your own relationships. Remember, like my grandfather's patient lessons or the connection I felt with Louis Armstrong's music, the most profound changes often start with small, intentional acts of understanding and appreciation.

These experiences illustrate that authentic relationships are built on compassion, nurtured through creative understanding, and deepened by shared moments that resonate deeply. As you reflect upon your own journey, remember that while our personal insights are invaluable, they're just the beginning.

Recent scientific research has uncovered fascinating physiological aspects of human bonding. We're now entering an exciting frontier -- the study of heart-brain coherence. By weaving together our lived experiences with these scientific insights, we can develop a richer understanding of how to create and nurture truly authentic relationships.

Heart-Brain Harmony

As we delve deeper into the foundations of authentic relationships, let's explore an exciting frontier in the science of connection through the fascinating work of acclaimed author and researcher Gregg Braden and the *HeartMath Institute*. This research offers us a new perspective on enhancing our relationships, reminding me of the profound connection I felt when I first heard Louis Armstrong play – a connection that seemed to resonate from his heart directly to mine.

The *HeartMath Institute* has discovered what they call "heart-brain coherence," which is a state where our heart rhythms and brain waves synchronize. When we're in this state, we're better able to manage our emotions, think clearly, and form deeper connections with others. It's like tuning an instrument to play in perfect harmony with others.

Dr. Rollin McCraty, Director of Research at *HeartMath Institute*, explains: *"The heart generates the largest electromagnetic field produced by the body. This field can be measured several feet away from the body and can affect those around us."*

Here's a simple technique to experience heart-brain coherence:

- **Heart Focus:** Direct your attention to your heart area.
- **Heart Breathing:** Imagine breathing deeply through your heart.
- **Heart Feeling:** Recall a positive feeling, like appreciation for someone in your life.

I'm reminded of how my father used to prepare for his "Officer Friendly" presentations. He would take a moment to center himself, much like this technique that allowed him to connect more authentically with the community.

Research shows that practicing heart coherence can lead to reduced stress and anxiety, improved emotional regulation, enhanced intuition and decision-making, better communication in relationships, and increased resilience.

To illustrate the power of heart-brain coherence, let's look at the story of Marcus, a high school teacher struggling with classroom management.

Case Study: Marcus the High School Teacher

Marcus had been teaching for five years, but his 10th-grade English class was pushing him to his limits. Disruptions were frequent, and he often left school feeling drained and discouraged. *"I was at my wit's end,"* Marcus recalls. *"I'd tried every classroom management technique in the book, but nothing seemed to work."*

Desperate for a solution, Marcus attended a workshop on heart-brain coherence. Skeptical at first, he decided to give it a try. Every morning before class, he practiced the *Quick Coherence Technique* we just learned.

"The first few days, I didn't notice much difference, but by the end of the week something had shifted. I felt calmer and more centered when I walked into the classroom."

As Marcus continued his practice, he noticed subtle changes in his students' behavior. They seemed more settled, more engaged. Disruptions decreased, and participation increased.

Dr. Elena Rivera, the Educational Psychologist who studied Marcus's classroom, observed, *"The change in the classroom atmosphere was palpable. Marcus's coherent state appeared to have a ripple effect on his students."* One student, Javier, who had been particularly challenging, approached Marcus after class one day. *"I don't know what's different, Mr. M, but I feel like you really see me now. It makes me want to try harder."*

Over the course of the semester, Marcus's class transformed. Test scores improved and several students reported enjoying English for the first time. Marcus reflected, *"By focusing on my own heart-brain coherence, I was able to connect with my students on a deeper level. It reminded me why I became a teacher in the first place."*

As you continue your journey of building authentic relationships, consider incorporating these heart-brain coherence techniques into your personal and professional life. Like my grandfather's patient financial lessons or the way Armstrong's music spoke to souls, this practice can help you create deeper, more resonant connections with others.

Remember, cultivating heart-brain coherence is a skill that grows with practice. Be patient with yourself as you explore these techniques. Over time, you may find they become a natural part of how you approach relationships, helping you create connections that are truly heart-to-heart.

Ubuntu: Connecting Through Shared Humanity

As we delve deeper into authentic relationships, let's explore *Ubuntu*, an African philosophy that beautifully complements our scientific understanding of connection. This concept reminds me of the collective spirit I witnessed in my father's community policing efforts and the musical synergy I felt listening to Louis Armstrong play with his band.

Ubuntu, a Nguni Bantu term often translated as "*I am because we are*," embodies our intrinsic interconnectedness. It aligns closely with what we've learned about heart-brain coherence and its ripple effects on those around us.

To illustrate the transformative power of Ubuntu, let me share the story of Themba, a young South African man.

Themba's Ubuntu Awakening

Themba, a young professional in Cape Town, had always prioritized personal success over community. His mindset was "*every man for himself*," a stark contrast to the Ubuntu philosophy of his ancestors.

When his elderly neighbor, Mama Zola, fell ill, Themba initially ignored it. But he soon noticed the community rallying around her. People cooked meals, cleaned her house, and accompanied her to doctor's appointments. What struck Themba most was the joy they found in helping.

Curious, Themba asked his childhood friend, Sipho, why he dedicated so much time to Mama Zola. Sipho smiled and said, "*Ubuntu, my brother. Mama Zola is part of us. Her wellbeing is our wellbeing.* This stirred something in Themba. Hesitantly at first, he began participating in Mama Zola's care. As days passed, Themba experienced a profound shift. He felt the joy of contributing to others' wellbeing and a deep sense of belonging he'd never known.

Themba's journey from individualism to embracing Ubuntu transformed not just his perspective, but also his relationships and sense of fulfillment. He discovered that success shared is success multiplied, and that true wealth lies in the strength of our connections to others.

Themba's journey teaches us key aspects of Ubuntu:

- **Interconnectedness:** Our actions and wellbeing are intertwined with others'.
- **Shared Humanity:** Recognizing others' humanity enhances our own.
- **Collective Wellbeing:** Community health is inseparable from individual health.
- **Empathy and Compassion:** Feeling and responding to others' experiences as if they were our own.
- **Reciprocity:** Uplifting others to uplift ourselves.

Ubuntu beautifully embodies our 3 C's:

Compassion: Caring deeply for others' wellbeing.

Creativity: Finding innovative ways to support our community.

Connection: Recognizing and nurturing our interconnectedness.

Dr. Nompumelelo Motlafi, a South African Political Scientist, explains: "*Ubuntu is not just a philosophy, but a practice of being human together. It's about recognizing that my humanity is caught up, is inextricably bound up, in yours.*"

As we integrate Ubuntu into our understanding of relationships, consider how viewing yourself as inherently connected to others changes your approach to relationships. What opportunities can you find to contribute to your community's wellbeing?

Remember, just as my grandfather's lessons on financial responsibility were about more than money – they were about care and connection

– Ubuntu is about more than just being nice. It's a profound recognition of our shared humanity and interdependence.

In the spirit of Ubuntu, when you thrive, we all thrive. As you continue to build authentic relationships, carry this wisdom with you. It's a beautiful framework for creating connections that are not just personal, but deeply human.

Vulnerability: Strength in Openness

As we continue to dive deeper into authentic relationships, let's explore vulnerability, which is a concept I first truly grasped as an actor. On stage, vulnerability is essential. It's the key to creating a powerful, genuine connection with the audience.

I vividly recall a performance where I had to tap into deeply personal grief. Standing there, emotions laid bare, I felt utterly exposed and alone. My hands trembled, my voice cracked. Yet in that moment of raw vulnerability, something magical happened. The audience leaned in. I saw tears in their eyes and felt their breath catch. We were no longer separate actor and viewers, but connected in a profound, almost spiritual way.

This, my friends, is the essence of vulnerability. It's scary, yes, but it's also the key that unlocks the door to genuine connection. Dr. Brené Brown, whom I deeply admire, puts it beautifully: *"Vulnerability is the birthplace of love, belonging, joy, courage, empathy, and creativity."* Her work shows us that when we dare to be vulnerable, we open ourselves to more fulfilling relationships and a stronger sense of self-worth.

But here's the thing! Being vulnerable isn't just about exposing our soft underbelly to the world. It starts with how we treat ourselves. Dr. Kristin Neff, another brilliant mind in this field, reminds us that *"Self-compassion provides the emotional safety needed to be vulnerable."* It's like creating a soft-landing place within us, making it easier to take those leaps of vulnerability with others.

So, why exactly is vulnerability so powerful? Let me break it down for you:

It's real: When we're vulnerable, we show up as our authentic selves with no masks and no pretenses.

It builds trust: Opening up creates a space for others to do the same, fostering mutual support.

It sparks empathy: Our vulnerability often encourages others to lower their guards too.

It fuels growth: Those moments of emotional risk are your springboard for personal development.

It deepens connections: Sharing our true fears and dreams creates intimacy like nothing else can.

Now, I know what you might be thinking. *"Bill, this sounds great, but how do I actually do this?"* Don't worry, I've got you. Here are some steps I've learned along the way:

Start small: Share a minor worry with a trusted friend.

Get real with your feelings: Next time someone asks how you are, try honestly responding.

Ask for help: It's not weakness, it's courage.

Share your dreams: Let people in on what really matters to you.

Take the compliment: A simple "thank you" goes a long way.

Own your mistakes: A sincere apology shows true strength.

Be kind to yourself: Treat yourself with the compassion you'd offer a dear friend.

Remember, vulnerability is like a muscle. The more you use it, the stronger it gets. It might feel uncomfortable at first, but trust me, the rewards are worth it.

As we've explored throughout this book, vulnerability beautifully embodies our 3 C's:

Compassion: It requires kindness towards us and invites receiving it from others.

Creativity: It opens us up to new ways of thinking and being.

Connection: It's the bridge that allows us to truly reach each other.

I'm reminded of something C.S. Lewis once said: *"To love at all is to be vulnerable."* Every time we choose to love, to connect, to show up as our true selves, we're choosing vulnerability. And in those moments, my friends, we find our greatest strength and our deepest connections.

So, I encourage you to embrace vulnerability in your life. Start small, be patient with yourself, and watch in wonder as your relationships deepen and your sense of self grows stronger.

Just as I learned on that stage years ago, it's in our most vulnerable moments that we often find our truest selves and our most profound connections.

Mastering Empathetic Communication

Let's talk about a superpower we all have but often forget to use – empathetic communication. Remember a time when you felt truly heard? When someone gave you their undivided attention, truly understanding where you were coming from? That feeling is magical, isn't it?

I first grasped the true power of empathetic communication on stage. As an actor, I learned that to truly connect with an audience, you needed to listen to the words, as well as the emotions behind them. It's a skill that's served me well beyond the footlights.

Dr. Carl Rogers, a pioneer in Humanistic Psychology, put it beautifully: *"When someone really hears you without passing judgment on you, without trying to take responsibility for you, without trying to mold you, it feels damn good!"* Ain't that the truth?

So why does this matter? When we communicate with empathy, we're essentially saying, *"I see you, I hear you, and what you say matters."* It's like shining a spotlight on someone's soul, making them feel valued and understood. And let me tell you, when people feel understood, they open up, trust more, and suddenly, your relationship is operating on a whole new level.

Again, you might be thinking, *"Bill, this sounds great, but how do I actually do this?"* I've got you covered. Here are some tricks of the trade:

Give full attention: Look them in the eyes. Put away that phone (yes, really!). Show them they're the star of your show right now.

Show you're listening: Nod, make those "mm-hmm" sounds. It's like applauding between acts and keeps the performance going.

Reflect back: Paraphrase what you've heard. It's like doing a scene replay to make sure you've got the script right.

Ask open-ended questions: Think of it as improv. *"How did that make you feel?"* or *"What happened next?"*

Avoid interrupting: Let them finish their monologue before you jump in with your lines.

Suspend judgment: Your job isn't to be the critic right now. Just take in the performance.

Hold off on advice: Sometimes, people just need an audience, not a director.

Let me share a personal experience that really drove this home for me. Early in my acting career, I was struggling with a particularly challenging role. I just couldn't connect with the character's emotions. My director, instead of barking orders, simply sat with me and listened as I talked through my frustrations.

His attentive presence and thoughtful questions led me to insights about the character I hadn't realized before, which improved my performance while showing me the transformative power of truly being heard.

You know, I've found these same skills invaluable off-stage too, in my work as a minister, as a coach, even in my everyday interactions. It's like having a Swiss Army knife for relationships.

Now, let's tie this back to our 3 C's:

Compassion: Empathetic communication is compassion in action. It's about truly caring for the other person's experience.

Creativity: Understanding someone else's perspective often requires some creative thinking. It's like stepping into a role you've never played before.

Connection: This is the heart of it all. Empathetic communication is about creating and deepening connections through understanding and validation.

So, here's your challenge. In your next conversation, try this out: Put aside your props and distractions, and turn off that internal monologue. Just listen, really listen. You'll be amazed at how this simple act can transform your interaction.

Remember, my friends, in the grand performance of life, we're all both actors and audience. By practicing empathetic communication, we create a standing ovation-worthy connection every single time. Now, that's what I call a showstopper!

3 C's in Action: Relationship Edition

As we've explored the foundations of authentic relationships, we've seen how our core principles of Compassion, Creativity, and Connection form the bedrock of meaningful bonds:

Compassion: In understanding the qualities of meaningful relationships and embracing the Ubuntu philosophy, we've seen how compassion forms the heart of connection. It's through compassionate understanding that we create safe spaces for vulnerability and practice empathetic communication.

Creativity: Building authentic relationships often requires thinking outside the box. We've explored creative ways to express ourselves, understand others, and bridge differences. The *HeartMath* techniques offer a creative approach to fostering connection on a physiological level.

Connection: Every concept we've covered, from the qualities of meaningful relationships to the power of vulnerability, ultimately serves to deepen our connections. We're learning to create bonds deeply rooted in mutual understanding and shared humanity.

As you begin to implement these ideas, remember that these 3 C's reinforce each other. Compassion opens the door to deeper connections, creativity helps us find new ways to express compassion, and our connections provide fertile ground for both compassion and creativity to flourish. By consciously integrating these principles as you build relationships, you're laying the groundwork for authentic, lasting bonds.

As we conclude our exploration of authentic relationships, let's reflect on the transformative journey we've undertaken. Building genuine connections isn't a destination, but an ongoing process that enriches our lives and those around us. As Dr. Brené Brown aptly puts it, *"Connection is why we're here; it is what gives purpose and meaning to our lives."*

Throughout this chapter, we've delved deeply into the foundations of authentic relationships, uncovering their critical role in our personal growth and well-being.

We've explored the intricate dynamics of meaningful connections, from understanding their key qualities to embracing vulnerability and practicing empathetic communication. This journey isn't just about improving our interactions, but rather it's about creating a more fulfilling and connected life.

REFLECTIONS - Chapter 4: Building Authentic Connections

Connection Assessment:

1. How deeply do you listen in conversations?
2. When do you feel most connected to others?
3. What barriers prevent authentic connection?
4. How vulnerable are you willing to be?
5. Which relationships need more attention?

Weekly Connection Tracker:

1. **Quality Conversations Monitor** □ Length of meaningful exchanges □ Topics beyond small talk □ Active listening moments □ Shared vulnerability instances
2. **Relationship Building Practice** □ New connections initiated □ Existing bonds strengthened □ Follow-up conversations □ Empathy opportunities taken
3. **Connection Depth Gauge Rate each significant interaction** (1-10): □ Presence level □ Emotional authenticity □ Mutual understanding □ Trust building

Implementation Tips:

- Focus on quality over quantity
- Practice being fully present
- Notice connection opportunities
- Track conversation patterns

REFLECTIONS - CHAPTER 4: BUILDING AUTHENTIC CONNECTIONS

Connections Your Connection Journey

Building authentic connections requires intention, courage, and practice. Use this space to explore your experiences with creating deeper, more meaningful relationships.

Journal Prompts:

- Describe a recent moment of genuine connection
- What helps you open up to others?
- When do you feel most heard and understood?
- How do your best relationships differ from others?

Connection Reflection: Consider a meaningful relationship in your life:

- What makes it special?
- How did it develop?
- What can you learn from it?

Space for Personal Insights:

Weekly Connection Intention: Choose one relationship to nurture this week:

How will you deepen this connection?

Remember: Every authentic connection starts with a single moment of genuine presence and openness. Small steps lead to profound relationships.

What lessons about connection from Chapter 4 resonated most?

COMING ATTRACTIONS

PLATINUM EDITION

THE PLATINUM REMIX

#1 SOULFUL HIT!

DEEPENING
AUTHENTIC BONDS

Featuring the Chart-Topping Hits:

"Vulnerability Groove" (Extended Mix)

"Empathy Echo" (Soul Version)

"The Trust-Building Bassline" (Remix)

DROPPING IN CHAPTER 5

5

DEEPENING AUTHENTIC BONDS

"The quality of your life is the quality of your relationships."
— Tony Robbins

Welcome back, friend. In the last chapter, we laid the groundwork for building authentic relationships. We explored the essential qualities that form the bedrock of meaningful connections, delved into the Ubuntu philosophy, embraced the power of vulnerability, and honed our empathetic communication skills.

Now, it's time to take things a step further. In this chapter, we'll explore how to nurture and strengthen these authentic connections we've begun to forge. Because here's the truth: building relationships is one thing, but maintaining and deepening them is an art in itself.

We're about to embark on a journey that will teach you how to set healthy boundaries, express gratitude in ways that truly resonate, practice forgiveness when it's tough, and overcome the inevitable challenges that arise in any meaningful relationship.

Just as a garden needs constant care to flourish, our relationships require ongoing attention and nurturing to reach their full potential. You'll glean practical strategies to keep your connections strong, resilient, and ever evolving. You'll also navigate the complexities of human interaction with grace and authenticity.

So, are you ready to take your relationships to new heights by creating connections that stand the test of time and grow richer and more fulfilling with each passing day.

Boundary Mastery

Think about the walls of your home. They keep you safe and they give you space. Just like walls, boundaries in relationships keep us safe and provide us with space. It's essential that every human being constructs these walls to make sure we are okay.

Allow me to guide you in building your walls through words and actions.

Dr. Henry Cloud and Dr. John Townsend, authors of the influential book *Boundaries*, explain: *"Boundaries define us. They define what is me and what is not me. A boundary shows me where I end and someone else begins, leading me to a sense of ownership."* This concept is particularly meaningful in order to maintain healthy relationships.

First, know what makes you happy and what does not. If someone wants to talk to you about something that makes you unhappy, then you have the right to say, "No." This 'no' is a small word, but it's a big wall. It tells others that you are taking care of yourself and keeping you safe.

Let's say you want to tell someone to recognize your boundary. Think about how you want to feel when you tell them. You want to feel calm, not angry or sad. Just calm because when you are calm, you can think better. You can say things better. So, find a time when you are calm to talk about your boundary.

Next, be clear. Say what you are okay with and what you are not. For example, you can say, *"I am okay with talking about work at home, but not after 8 PM."* It tells the other person precisely what your boundaries are.

After you define for someone your boundaries, you need to stick to them. If you fail to do this, it's like having a hole in your wall where unwanted items can penetrate it at will. When you replace indecisiveness with a definite stance, you keep your wall strong.

Sometimes, someone might not like your boundaries. These people might try to change your mind. But remember, your wall is there to keep you safe. You do not have to change it if you don't want to. It's okay to keep your wall up. If someone keeps trying to change your mind, you can say, *"I told you how I feel. My mind is not changing."* Affirming your boundaries is how you take care of your wall.

But what if you have a wall that is too big? What if you respond negatively to everything and everyone? Well, then you might miss out on fun things, or worse, things that are key to your well-being. So, check your walls now and then. Make sure they are not too big or too small. You want walls that keep you safe, but also let the good things in.

Setting boundaries is an act of self-compassion, one of our core C's. It's also a creative process, as you find unique ways to express your needs. And ironically, clear boundaries lead to stronger connections, as they foster respect and understanding in relationships.

To be clear, your boundaries are not meant to push people away, but to create a safe space where authentic connections can flourish. By setting clear boundaries, you're actually inviting people to connect with the real you.

The Gratitude Effect

Expressing gratitude and appreciation is a powerful way to strengthen relationships, making others feel valued and fostering positivity. Dr. Robert Emmons, a leading expert on gratitude, found that expressing gratitude can significantly improve well-being and relationships. He states, *"Gratitude is the ultimate touchpoint of human-to-human interaction. It dissolves negative feelings; it loosens our grip on toxic emotions, and it amplifies the good."*

Gratitude is like a warm hug with words. It's telling someone, *"I see what you did, and it means a lot."* It's a simple way to make someone's day better, which in turn makes you feel good. This creates a happiness circle that keeps going around and around.

Appreciation, on the other hand, is about recognizing the bigger picture. It's like looking at a painting and seeing all the colors and shapes that make it beautiful. When you appreciate someone, you say, *"I see all the good things you bring to my life."*

Daily Practices

Incorporating gratitude into your daily life can be transformative. Here are some practical ways to express gratitude and appreciation:

Start your day with a thankful thought. Before getting out of bed, think of one thing you're grateful for. It sets a positive tone for the day.

Write "thank you" notes. Do this, not just for gifts, but also for small acts of kindness. Did a friend listen to you when you had a rough day? Write the friend a note.

Say thanks to people you see every day. Pay attention to the bus driver or the barista. Look them in the eye and express sincere gratitude for all they do.

Give compliments. If you see someone wearing a nice hat or hear someone singing a lovely tune, let them know.

Don't forget family and close friends. Tell them how much you appreciate them, not just on special occasions, but routinely.

End your day with reflection. Think about what went well and find something to be thankful for before going to sleep.

Impact on Relationships

Expressing gratitude and appreciation strengthens bonds and fosters positivity. When you tell someone you're grateful, it lights up something inside them. They feel noticed and valued, which can only make the bond between you stronger. It's like glue that not only sticks you together, but also makes you want to stick together.

Integrating the 3 C's

Expressing gratitude and appreciation beautifully embodies the 3 C's:

Compassion: Expressing gratitude is an act of kindness, showing that you care about others and their efforts.

Creativity: Finding new and sincere ways to express thanks is a creative endeavor, keeping your relationships fresh and vibrant.

Connection: Realizing how gratitude strengthens bonds between people, deepening your connections and fostering a positive cycle of appreciation.

Remember that saying thanks and showing appreciation take you beyond politeness to producing a way of living. It's a choice to be kind and to appreciate the good around you. When you do that, you're improving your world one "thank you" at a time.

Forgiveness: The Path to Freedom

Forgiveness is a cornerstone of emotional and psychological well-being, offering earnest benefits for individuals and communities. At its essence, forgiveness is the conscious decision to release feelings of resentment or vengeance toward someone who has harmed you, regardless of whether they deserve your forgiveness.

Dr. Frederic Luskin, Director of the Stanford University Forgiveness Projects, explains, *"Forgiveness is the experience of peacefulness in the present moment. Forgiveness does not change the past, but it enlarges the future."* His research shows that practicing forgiveness can lead to increased optimism, reduced anger, and improved physical health.

Giving people the space to make mistakes is necessary to cultivate meaningful relationships. People have complex lives filled with responsibilities and pressures outside of their relationship with us. There will be moments when they fall short of our expectations, fail to honor a promise they made, or act in a way that makes us feel like we don't matter. Everyone makes mistakes, and when given the room to self-reflect, people will most often acknowledge their wrongs and have that recognition mold their future behavior.

The first step to embracing forgiveness is being willing to forgive ourselves. If we are not charitable in our self-perception, if the standards that govern what we consider appropriate behavior are too high, then we will never be able to practice forgiveness when it comes to our relationship with others.

If you ever make a mistake, fall short of a standard you set for yourself, or fail at something you tried, do not hold it against yourself. Acknowledge your error, but don't let it consume you. If you did something wrong, affirm its wrongness, but do so in a way where you are lenient with yourself. Say, *"I shouldn't have done that, but that does not reflect who I am."*

Forgiveness fosters emotional healing. Holding onto grudges and anger can lead to prolonged stress and mental health issues such as anxiety and depression. By forgiving, individuals let go of negative emotions, reducing stress and improving their overall mental health. This process leads to increased feelings of peace, happiness, and well-being.

When it comes to forgiving others, remember that forgiveness is not about condoning hurtful behavior or forgetting what happened. It's about freeing yourself from the burden of resentment and anger.

Here are some steps to practice forgiveness:

Acknowledge the hurt. Recognize and validate your feelings about what happened.

Consider the other person's perspective. Try to understand what you might have done to precipitate their actions.

Choose to forgive. Make a conscious decision to let go of resentment.

Release the negative emotions. This might involve journaling, talking to a friend, or seeking professional help.

Redefine your relationship. Decide how you want to move forward, which may or may not involve reconciliation.

Forgiveness doesn't always mean reconciliation. Sometimes, forgiveness is about finding peace within yourself, regardless of whether the relationship continues.

Let's tie this back to our 3 C's:

Compassion: Forgiveness is a profound act of compassion, both for others and for us.

Creativity: Finding ways to forgive often requires creative thinking, especially in complex situations.

Connection: Forgiveness can heal and strengthen our connections, thereby allowing for deeper, more authentic relationships.

Don't forget that forgiveness is a process, not a one-time event. It takes practice and patience. But the freedom and peace it brings to our relationships and our lives makes it a worthwhile journey.

Navigating Relationship Hurdles

Building and maintaining authentic relationships isn't always a "walk in the park." You might fear vulnerability, struggle with trust issues, or find it difficult to make time for meaningful connections in your busy life. But here's the thing -- these challenges are where the real growth happens.

Take Daryl Davis, for example. This African American musician didn't only face a challenge in building connections, but he also faced a chasm of hatred and prejudice. But Daryl, with a heart full of courage and curiosity, reached out to members of the *Ku Klux Klan*. Can you imagine the fear he must have felt? The doubts that must have crept in? But Daryl persisted, driven by a belief in the power of authentic connection.

Through genuine conversations and unwavering respect, Daryl formed unlikely friendships that led many Klan members to hang up their robes for good. His story is certainly inspiring. It's a masterclass in overcoming seemingly insurmountable challenges in building connections. It shows us that with patience, understanding, and a willingness to see the humanity in others, we can bridge even the widest divides.

Now, I'm not saying you need to go out and befriend extremists. But Daryl's example reminds us that the challenges we face in building authentic relationships, be it fear, mistrust, or differences in beliefs, can be overcome. It's about taking that first brave step, just as Daryl did, and being open to the transformative power of genuine connection.

While most of us won't face challenges as extreme as Daryl's, we all encounter obstacles in our journey to build and maintain authentic relationships. Let's explore some common challenges and strategies to overcome them:

Fear of Vulnerability: Being vulnerable isn't a weakness, it's a strength. Start small. Share a little more of yourself each time you interact with someone. If you're afraid of judgment, remind yourself that authentic relationships are built on acceptance, not perfection.

Trust Issues: Trust is built over time through consistent, positive interactions. If you've been hurt before, it's natural to be cautious. However, giving someone a chance doesn't mean letting your guard down completely. Take small steps and allow trust to grow organically.

Time Constraints: In our busy lives, it's easy to neglect our relationships. Remember, quality often matters more than quantity. Even brief, genuine interactions can nurture a relationship. Schedule regular check-ins with important people in your life, even if it's just a quick call or message.

Misunderstandings and Conflicts: Disagreements are normal in any relationship. The key is how you handle them. Practice active listening, express your feelings using "I" statements, and focus on finding solutions together rather than placing blame.

Maintaining Long-Distance Relationships: Distance can make connection challenging, but it's not impossible. Use technology to stay in touch, plan regular virtual dates, and find creative ways to share experiences despite the distance.

Dealing with Differences: Embracing diversity in relationships is challenging but rewarding. Approach differences with curiosity rather than judgment. See them as opportunities to learn and grow.

Dr. John Gottman, known for his work on marital stability, suggests that successful relationships aren't about avoiding conflicts but about how we navigate through them. He emphasizes the importance of "turning towards" each other during challenging times, rather than turning away or against each other.

For each of these challenges, consider how you can apply the 3 C's:

Compassion: Practice self-compassion when you struggle and extend compassion to others who might be facing similar challenges.

Creativity: Think outside the box to find innovative solutions to relationship obstacles. Get creative in how you connect, resolve conflicts, or express your feelings.

Connection: Remember that working through challenges together can actually deepen your connection. Every obstacle overcome is an opportunity for a stronger bond.

Here's a practical exercise to help you tackle relationship challenges. First, identify a current challenge in one of your relationships. Write down how this challenge makes you feel. Brainstorm at least two creative ways you could address this challenge. Choose one approach to try, keeping compassion for yourself and the other person in mind.

After trying your chosen approach, reflect on how it impacted your connection. Comfort yourself by knowing that building authentic relationships is a journey, not a destination. It's okay to stumble sometimes. What matters is that you keep trying, keep learning, and keep opening your heart to meaningful connections.

As we conclude our exploration of nurturing and strengthening authentic connections, let's reflect on the transformative journey we've undertaken. Remember, building deep, meaningful relationships isn't a one-time achievement, but an ongoing process that continually enriches our lives. As Psychiatrist Dr. Irvin Yalom said, *"It's the relationship that heals, the relationship that heals, the relationship that heals."*

Throughout this chapter, we've analyzed the heart of authentic connections, uncovering their critical role in our personal growth and well-being. We've explored the intricate "dance" of establishing boundaries, extending gratitude and forgiveness, and overcoming challenges in our relationships. This journey is about improving our interactions in order to create a foundation for a more fulfilling, connected life.

REFLECTIONS - CHAPTER 5: DEEPENING AUTHENTIC BONDS

Relationship Assessment:

1. How are your boundaries serving you currently?
2. Where do your connections need strengthening?
3. What patterns do you notice in your relationships?
4. How do you handle relationship challenges?
5. What makes your strongest relationships work?

Weekly Relationship Tracker:

1. Boundary Practice ▢ Clear boundaries set ▢ Boundaries respected/challenged ▢ Difficult conversations had ▢ Self-advocacy moments ▢ Energy levels after interactions
2. Connection Deepening ▢ Meaningful conversations ▢ Active listening practiced ▢ Vulnerability shared ▢ Support offered/received ▢ Quality time invested
3. Trust Building ▢ Promises kept ▢ Reliability demonstrated ▢ Understanding shown ▢ Forgiveness practiced ▢ Trust tested/strengthened

Implementation Tips:

- Start with one relationship focus
- Practice consistent boundary setting
- Notice relationship patterns
- Document what strengthens bonds

REFLECTIONS - Chapter 5: Deepening Authentic Bonds

Your Relationship Journey

Building deeper connections requires intention, courage, and wisdom. Use this space to explore your relationship patterns, challenges, and growth opportunities.

Journal Prompts:

- Which relationship has grown strongest lately? Why?
- What relationship patterns would you like to change?
- How do you show up differently with different people?
- Where do you need to establish better boundaries?

Connection Reflection:

- What makes you feel truly seen and heard?
- How do you help others feel understood?
- What relationship habits serve you well?
- Which relationships need more attention?

Space for Growth Insights:

Weekly Relationship Intention: Choose one relationship to mindfully nurture this week:

What will you do differently?

Remember: Deep connections grow through consistent care, clear boundaries, and authentic expression. Each interaction is an opportunity to strengthen your bonds.

What key relationship insights emerged from Chapter 5?

COMING ATTRACTIONS

6

IGNITING YOUR CREATIVE SPARK

"Creativity is intelligence having fun."
— Albert Einstein

Creativity Decoded

Creativity is an inherent part of the human experience, extending far beyond the realms of art, music, and dance. Each of us possesses a unique blend of creativity shaped by our preferences, experiences, education, upbringing, and circumstances. This diversity is evident in the choices we make and the lives we lead, painting a rich tapestry of human existence.

As we explore the concept of creativity, I'm reminded of my transformative experience with Louis Armstrong's music. That moment was magical to awakening in me an appreciation of great jazz. But beyond that, it was a powerful demonstration of how creativity can inspire and ignite passion in others. Armstrong's innovative approach to trumpet playing and his unique improvisational style exemplify the kind of creativity we're discussing. He took existing musical forms and transformed them, creating something new and deeply moving.

This is precisely the kind of creative thinking we can apply in various aspects of our lives. Moreover, that experience showcased how a single creative act can have far-reaching effects because Armstrong's creativity in one performance sparked my lifelong passion for music, influencing my career and approach to problem-solving. It's a testament to how creativity can be a catalyst for personal growth and transformation.

The Creative Brain

Dr. Mihaly Csikszentmihalyi, known for his research on creativity and flow, offers keen insights into how creativity impacts our well-being. In his book, *Creativity: Flow and the Psychology of Discovery and Invention*, he shows that creativity is about making art or solving problems, and it's also a way of engaging with life that makes us feel more fulfilled and purposeful.

Csikszentmihalyi's concept of flow describes a state where you're so absorbed in what you're doing that you lose track of time and self-consciousness. His studies show that we're at our happiest and most productive when we're in this flow state. And guess what? We often hit this sweet spot when we're being creative.

According to Csikszentmihalyi, creativity can manifest in how we approach our work, our relationships, and even our daily routines. By cultivating creativity in all aspects of life, we increase our capacity for innovation, problem-solving, and personal growth.

To tap into your creative potential and experience flow, Csikszentmihalyi suggests this:

- Choose activities that challenge you slightly beyond your current abilities.
- Set clear goals for what you want to achieve.

- Eliminate distractions and create an environment conducive to focus.
- Pay attention to the process, not just the end result.
- Lose yourself in the activity, letting go of self-consciousness and time awareness.

By regularly engaging in activities that induce flow, you will enhance your creativity and overall sense of well-being.

Creativity in Daily Life

Creativity can be found in countless aspects of our lives. Whether you're solving a complex problem at work, finding a new way to connect with a loved one, or reimagining your daily routine, you're tapping into your creative spirit. Here's how you do that:

Household Innovations: Reimagine your living space to maximize functionality. Try using multi-functional furniture, vertical storage solutions, and creative lighting to transform a cramped apartment into a cozy, efficient home. Think about how you might apply these ideas to your own space to enhance your daily living experience?

Parenting Hacks: Develop innovative ways to keep your children engaged and learning. Consider creating educational games from household items or organizing scavenger hunts that teach math and science concepts. What creative parenting strategies can you implement to enrich your children's learning?

Creativity in Professional Settings

Workplace Efficiency: Streamline your workflow by creating a custom digital dashboard that integrates all your tasks, emails, and schedules. Consider how you can use technology to boost your productivity and reduce stress at work?

Team Collaboration: Introduce brainstorming sessions where team members are encouraged to share wild ideas without judgment. How can you establish or become part of a culture of innovation and collaboration in your workplace or community?

Creative Approaches to Health and Wellness

Fitness Routines: Design a unique exercise routine that combines elements of dance, yoga, and strength training. How can you make your workouts more enjoyable and effective by incorporating different physical activities into them?

Healthy Eating: Try experimenting with new recipes that use different ingredients and cooking techniques from whatever you're used to. How can you turn healthy eating into an exciting culinary adventure in your kitchen?

Community and Social Impact

Neighborhood Projects: Organize a neighborhood beautification project, encouraging residents to plant gardens, paint murals, and create public art installations. How do you think you can contribute to your community's identity and values through creative initiatives?

Social Initiatives: You could start a local initiative to address food insecurity by setting up community fridges stocked with surplus food from local businesses and donations. I admit that this idea could be more time-consuming than you wish to commit, but what social challenges in your community could you creatively address?

As we explore the various facets of creativity, let's turn our attention to a powerful form of creative expression that permeates nearly every aspect of our lives -- music. This universal language not only showcases human creativity at its finest, but it also serves as a wellspring of inspiration for countless other creative endeavors.

The fact is that music surrounds us constantly, from the background melodies in grocery stores to the tunes that greet us when we're put on hold. This ubiquity is no accident.

Music possesses a unique, almost mystical ability to influence our moods, spark our imaginations, and fuel our creativity across various domains.

Moreover, music has an uncanny way of meeting us exactly where we are emotionally. How often have you experienced a moment where the perfect song comes on at just the right time, as if by magic? It provides comfort or motivation, or maybe a sense of connection when you need it most.

This remarkable quality of music, which is its ability to resonate with our deepest feelings and experiences, makes it a powerful catalyst for creativity and emotional expression.

When I first "dipped my toes" into the creative world, it was through music. And let me tell you that it opened up a whole new universe of expression and connection that I never knew existed. As we go deeper into the creative aspects of music, consider how it embodies all 3 C's:

Compassion in its ability to comfort and unite; **Creativity** in its endless forms of expression; and **Connection** in its power to bring people together across all boundaries.

By exploring music as a form of creativity, we can gain insights into the broader creative process and how it intertwines with compassion and connection. Let's discover how this extraordinary art form can inspire and enhance our creative pursuits in all areas of life.

The Universal Language of Connection and Creativity

Music is often called the universal language, and for good reason. It has this incredible ability to transcend barriers of language, culture, and even time. Dr. Stefan Koelsch, famous Neuroscientist specializing in music, has found that music activates almost every region of our brain. It's like a full-body workout for our grey matter!

But here's where it gets really interesting. Music doesn't just light up our individual brains, but it also has the power to synchronize brains across a group of people. When we listen to music together, our brains actually start to sync up. It's a phenomenon called "neural entrainment." Essentially, our brainwaves begin to match the rhythm of the music and, by extension, match each other's. This shared experience creates a powerful sense of connection and belonging.

Here are a few ways you can use music to boost your creativity and connection:

Active Listening: Focus on a piece of music. Notice the different instruments, the rhythm, and the emotions it evokes.

Music and Movement: Put on some music and let your body move freely. This releases creative blocks and connect you more deeply with your emotions.

Collaborative Playlists: Create a shared playlist with friends or family. It's a fun way to express yourself and learn about others.

Music Journaling: Write about the memories or feelings that certain songs evoke. This can be a powerful tool for self-reflection and creative inspiration.

Carving Out Creative Time

Life moves fast. There's always something to do. You wake up, and before you know it, you're ready for bed again. Where did the time go? Often, you think about painting, writing, or just doodling. But where is the time? Well, it's there. You just need to look for it.

Setting aside time for creativity is like saving money. As you might put a little money away with each paycheck, do the same with time. This time becomes your investment in yourself, your very own creative fund. Think about it. You save up for things you value. So, shouldn't you save time for something as valuable as your creativity?

Now, how do you carve out this time? Let's get practical. Look at your day. Find a small pocket of time. It might be only fifteen minutes. That's fine. Start there. Wake up a little earlier or cut down on the time you watch shows. Everyone has the same twenty-four hours. It's all about how you use them.

Once you find this precious time, make it a no-judgment zone. It's not about making a masterpiece. It's about the joy of creating. You could scribble, throw paint on canvas, or mash keys on a keyboard and make up stories. The point is to let go without expectations. Just you and your creativity hanging out together.

Problem-Solving: The Creative Way

Creative problem-solving helps you tackle challenges that don't have simple answers. Sometimes, life throws us a curveball, but the usual ways of fixing things don't work. That's when being creative with addressing our problems can surface. It's about looking at a situation from all sides and coming up with answers that no one has thought of before, especially you!

To grow this skill, try these four ideas:

Be Curious: Ask why things are the way they are. Look for answers. Dig deep.

Think Outside the Box: Consider your problem in ways you've never thought of before. Ask, "What if?" questions.

Brainstorm: Write down your problem and all the ideas you have around them. No idea is a bad idea. Just let them flow.

Test Your Ideas: Choose one idea that seems good and try it out. Learn from each attempt and refine your approach.

Creativity: A Collaborative Affair

Working with others on something creative is incredibly rewarding. It's like putting together a puzzle. Everyone has their pieces, and when you join them, you see a big, beautiful picture. When you share a creative goal with someone else, something special emerges. You find new friends, and you learn about them, and they learn about you.

To find the right people to work or socialize with, look for those who share your interests. Plan regular meetings and share your thoughts. Celebrate differences and learn from each other. Collaboration can inspire future creative work and help you learn new skills.

Celebrating Creative Wins

When you make something, it feels good. It's important to celebrate your wins, no matter how small. Tell a friend or family member about what you made. Share it on social media if you like. The point is to let others see your work. It's not showing off; it's sharing your joy.

Keep a record of what you make, like a diary for your creations. Write down what you did and how you felt. When you look back, you'll see how far you've come. And that's something to celebrate.

Crushing Creative Blocks

As you embark on rediscovering your creative spirit, you might encounter self-doubt, fear of judgment, or the dreaded "creativity block." These challenges are common, even among experienced creatives.

When self-doubt creeps in, remind yourself that creativity isn't about perfection, but expression and exploration. Give yourself permission to create without judgment. If you're afraid of others' opinions, start by creating just for yourself. You don't have to share anything you make.

If you hit a creativity block, try changing your environment, taking a walk, or engaging in a different creative activity. Sometimes, stepping away and returning with fresh eyes can reignite your creativity.

Remember that creativity is like a muscle -- the more you use it, the stronger it becomes. Be patient with yourself and celebrate small creative acts. Over time, you'll find your creative confidence growing. The path to creativity isn't always smooth. However, it's often through overcoming these challenges that the most inspiring breakthroughs occur.

Let's now turn our attention to some remarkable examples of creativity in action. These stories demonstrate how individuals have successfully navigated obstacles to bring their innovative ideas to life, showcasing the transformative power of creative thinking.

Creativity Champions

Creativity is about more than making art. It's about seeing the world in new ways and finding innovative solutions. Let's look at some inspiring examples that show us how creativity can change lives and spark positive change:

Mexican artist, *Frida Kahlo*, turned her personal struggles into powerful works of art. Despite facing numerous health challenges, Kahlo used her creativity to express her pain, dreams, and cultural identity through vibrant self-portraits and paintings. Her story reminds us that creativity can be a powerful tool for self-expression and healing, even in the face of adversity.

Pixar Animation Studios has revolutionized storytelling through animation. Their creative process involves collaboration, risk-taking, and constant innovation. From *Toy Story* to *Inside Out*, Pixar's films touch hearts and spark imaginations worldwide.

Margaret, a 68-year-old retiree, discovered her creative spirit in a community art class. She began making beautiful sculptures from recycled materials while raising awareness about environmental issues and inspiring her community to think differently about waste.

Jason, a 35-year-old veteran, found solace in art therapy. Through abstract paintings, he expressed emotions he couldn't verbalize at first, but gradually, he enjoyed healing and connecting with other veterans on similar journeys.

Aisha, a first-generation immigrant, blended cuisines from her homeland with local ingredients to create a unique fusion restaurant that brought her community together and celebrated cultural diversity.

These diverse examples above show that persons open to utilizing their creativity in a myriad of ways can thrive in various settings.

They ended up solving problems, healing wounds, bridging cultures, and driving innovation when nurtured with openness and persistence.

3 C's Fusion: Creative Edition

As we nurture our creativity, it's important to remember how it intertwines with compassion and connection. Creative acts are a powerful way to express compassion and forge deeper connections with others.

For example, you might use your creativity to craft a thoughtful gift for a friend in need, or to develop an innovative solution to a community problem.

Consider starting a creative project that focuses on spreading kindness or building community. This could be anything, from writing uplifting messages to leave in public places, to organizing a collaborative art installation that brings neighbors together. By intentionally infusing your creative pursuits with compassion and connection, you'll not only enhance your own well-being, but you'll also contribute positively to those around you.

Creativity is most certainly personal expression. Additionally, it's a powerful tool for building empathy, understanding others' perspectives, and creating meaningful connections.

As you explore your creative spirit, look for opportunities to use your creativity as a bridge to connect with others and show compassion in innovative ways.

As we conclude our exploration of creativity, let's review the transformative journey we've embarked upon. Rediscovering your creative spirit isn't a one-time event. No, it's an ongoing adventure that continually enriches our lives. As Albert Einstein wisely observed, *"Creativity is intelligence having fun."*

Throughout this chapter, we've explored in depth the wellspring of creativity, uncovering its critical role in personal growth, problem-solving, and self-expression. We've explored the landscape of our creative potential from everyday innovations to artistic pursuits.

This journey of creative rediscovery is so much more than making art. It's about cultivating a mindset that enhances every aspect of our lives.

REFLECTIONS - Chapter 6: Igniting Your Creative Spark

Creativity Assessment:

1. When do your best ideas come to you?
2. What environments spark your creativity?
3. How do you currently solve problems?
4. What blocks your creative flow?
5. Which creative activities energize you?

Weekly Creativity Tracker:

1. **Creative Flow Monitor** □ Moments of inspiration □ Time spent in creative activities □ Flow state experiences □ Energy levels during creation
2. **Innovation Practice** □ New approaches tried □ Problems solved creatively □ Novel ideas generated □ Unique connections made
3. **Creative Expression** □ Creative risks taken □ New skills attempted □ Collaborative creations □ Playful experiments

Implementation Tips:

- Schedule daily creative time
- Embrace imperfection
- Document all ideas, even small ones
- Notice what sparks inspiration

REFLECTIONS - Chapter 6: Igniting Your Creative Spark

Your Creative Journey

Creativity isn't just about art—it's about seeing the world with fresh eyes and finding new ways to approach life's challenges. Use this space to explore and expand your creative potential.

Journal Prompts:

- What would you create if you couldn't fail?
- How do you feel during moments of creation?
- What childhood creative activities did you love?
- Where do you want to express more creativity?

Creativity Catalysts:

- List activities that inspire you
- Note times you felt most innovative
- Record creative dreams or visions
- Describe ideal creating conditions

Space for Creative Expression:

Weekly Creative Challenge: Choose one new creative experiment this week:

Remember: Creativity flourishes in an atmosphere of playfulness and permission. Give yourself space to explore, experiment, and even "fail" as you develop your creative abilities.

What creative insights emerged from Chapter 6?

Your consciousness will never be the same...

EXPAND YOUR MIND
MINDFULNESS MASTERY

"Where every moment becomes extraordinary"

WITNESS THE IMPOSSIBLE:

CONSCIOUSNESS-BENDING AWARENESS
"Reality will never look the same!"

HIGH-DEFINITION PRESENCE
"Every breath is a plot twist!"

MIND-ALTERING INSIGHTS
"Your perception will be revolutionized!"

"An IMAX experience for your consciousness!"

- MINDFUL OBSERVER

CHAPTER 7

7

MINDFULNESS MASTERY

"The present moment is filled with joy and happiness.
If you are attentive, you will see it."
— Thich Nhat Hanh

Intentional Mornings

When the sun peeks over the horizon, and the world stirs awake, it represents a new opportunity. It's the start of a new day, and **we** are in charge. But how often do we truly experience these moments? How often are we fully present in our own lives? This is where mindfulness comes in.

> *Mindfulness is about being fully present in the moment, aware of where we are and what we're doing, without being overly reactive or overwhelmed by what's going on around us.*

It's a simple concept, but it's not always easy to achieve in our fast-paced, constantly connected world.

"Mindfulness 101"

Dr. Jon Kabat-Zinn, the founder of Mindfulness-Based Stress Reduction, explains that mindfulness is *"paying attention in a particular way: on purpose, in the present moment, and non-judgmentally."*

It's not about clearing your mind of all thoughts or achieving a state of eternal calm. Instead, it's about observing your thoughts and feelings without judgment, allowing them to come and go without getting caught up in them.

Picture yourself sitting on the soft, grassy bank of a lively river. As you look at the glistening water, you notice how it reflects the sunlight and appears almost like liquid glass. This river represents the ongoing stream of your thoughts and feelings continually in motion.

The practice of mindfulness is akin to being seated there, quietly observing the water as it flows past, without feeling the urge to jump in or to try to stop its movement. You fully acknowledge the presence of the river, yet its currents don't sway you from your peaceful state of observation.

Mindfulness Roadblocks Cleared

You might be thinking, *"This sounds great, but I'm too busy. I don't have time for mindfulness."* It's a common concern in our fast-paced world. But here's the thing: mindfulness isn't about adding one more task to your to-do list. It's about approaching your existing activities with a different mindset.

Do you realize that mindfulness can be practiced in small moments throughout your day? You don't need to set aside hours for meditation unless you want to. Even a few mindful breaths while waiting for your coffee to brew, or a moment of awareness while brushing your teeth can make a difference.

As Jon Kabat-Zinn says, *"You don't have time to meditate? What about the time you spend worrying, ruminating, or caught up in negative thinking? That's the time to meditate."*

Start small. You might find that these brief moments of mindfulness actually create more time in your day by helping you focus better and reduce stress. As you experience the benefits, you may naturally want to dedicate more time to the practice.

The Mindful Brain

You might wonder, *"Does this really work?"* Well, science says it does! Research has shown that regular mindfulness practice can reduce stress, improve focus, and even change the structure of our brains.

Dr. Sara Lazar, Neuroscientist at *Harvard Medical School*, conducted groundbreaking research using brain scans. She found that mindfulness meditation can actually increase the cortical thickness in the hippocampus, which governs learning and memory. It also affects areas of the brain involved in emotional regulation and self-referential processing.

In simpler terms, mindfulness can help you learn better, remember more, manage your emotions more effectively, and gain a clearer perspective on yourself. Not bad for something you can practice anywhere, anytime, with no special equipment!

Mindfulness Toolkit

Now that we understand what mindfulness is and why it's beneficial, let's explore some basic techniques you can start using today:

Mindful Breathing: This is the foundation of many mindfulness practices. Find a comfortable position and focus your attention on your breath. Notice the sensation of the air moving in and out of your body. When your mind wanders, and it will, gently bring your attention back to your breath.

Body Scan Meditation: Lie down or sit comfortably and slowly focus your attention on different parts of your body, from your toes to the top of your head. Notice any sensations, emotions, or thoughts associated with each part of your body.

Mindful Walking: As you walk, pay attention to the sensation of your feet touching the ground, the movement of your legs, and the rhythm of your breath. Notice the sights, sounds, and smells around you.

Loving-Kindness Meditation: This practice involves directing positive thoughts and well-wishes to yourself and others. Start by focusing on yourself, then extend these thoughts to a loved one, an acquaintance, a difficult person, and finally to all beings.

Dadirri: Ancient Mindfulness Wisdom

As we explore mindfulness, it's valuable to consider diverse cultural perspectives that can enrich our understanding and practice. The Australian Aboriginal concept of 'dadirri' offers a profound approach to mindfulness that has been cultivated over thousands of years.

Dadirri, a word from the Ngan'gikurunggurr and Ngen'giwumirri languages of the Aboriginal people in the Daly River region, encompasses the practices of deep listening and quiet stillness. It's a form of contemplation that goes beyond mere meditation, embodying a way of being that is deeply connected to the land, community, and inner wisdom.

Miriam-Rose Ungunmerr-Baumann, an Aboriginal elder, artist, and educator, describes dadirri as "inner deep listening and quiet still awareness." She explains, *"It is something like what you call 'contemplation'... A big part of dadirri is listening."*

To understand dadirri, consider the story of Jake, a non-Indigenous Australian who spent time learning from Aboriginal elders in Arnhem Land. Jake was accustomed to the fast-paced life of Sydney, where he was always busy, always planning for the next thing. When he first arrived in the Aboriginal community, he found the slow pace and long silences uncomfortable.

One day, an elder invited Jake to sit by the river. They sat in silence for what felt like hours to Jake. He fidgeted, his mind racing with thoughts and questions. The elder gently instructed him, *"Listen to the river. Listen to the birds. Listen to your heartbeat. Just listen."*

As days passed, Jake began to understand. He learned to sit in stillness, to listen, not just with his ears, but also with his whole being. He noticed the subtle changes in the wind, the rhythms of nature, and the whispers of his own heart. This practice of dadirri helped Jake become more present, more aware, and more connected to himself and his surroundings.

The practice of dadirri teaches us several key aspects of mindfulness:

Deep Listening: This involves listening, not only to external sounds, but also to the wisdom within us, and the subtle messages from our environment.

Patience: Dadirri emphasizes the value of taking time and not rushing. It's about allowing understanding to come in its own time.

Quiet Stillness: This stillness is active, not passive. It's a state of heightened awareness and receptivity.

Connection: Dadirri fosters a deep sense of connection to nature, community, and oneself.

Reflection: It encourages deep contemplation and reflection on experiences and knowledge.

As we continue our exploration of mindfulness, consider how you could incorporate the wisdom of Dadirri into your daily life. Can you find moments for deep listening and quiet stillness? How might this practice enhance your awareness and connection to yourself and the world around you?

Mindful Living: Daily Practices

Mindfulness isn't only to be experienced on meditation cushions or yoga mats. You can bring mindfulness into every aspect of your daily life, and here are some ways to do that:

Mindful Eating: Instead of scarfing down your meals while scrolling through your phone, try eating without distractions. Pay attention to the flavors, textures, and smells of your food. Notice the sensation of lifting your fork, chewing, and swallowing.

Mindful Communication: When talking with others, give them your full attention. Listen to understand, not just to respond. Notice your own reactions and emotions during conversations.

Mindful Work Practices: Take short "mindful breaks" throughout your workday. Spend a few minutes focusing on your breath or doing a quick body scan. When working on tasks, give each of them your full attention, rather than multitasking.

Mindful Technology Use: Be aware of how and when you use technology. Before checking your phone or opening social media, pause and take a breath. Ask yourself if this is really how you want to spend your time and attention right now.

While these individual practices are powerful, consider envisioning the impact of integrating mindfulness on a larger scale. Let's explore a remarkable example of how mindfulness can transform entire communities when introduced systematically.

Classroom Calm: Mindfulness in Schools

Let's take a journey across the pond to the United Kingdom, where a simple idea has blossomed into a movement that's changing the lives of thousands of young people. This is the story of the Mindfulness in Schools Project (MiSP). It's a shining example of how bringing mindfulness into our daily lives can have far-reaching effects.

It all began in 2007 with two schoolteachers, Richard Burnett and Chris Cullen. They had personally experienced the benefits of mindfulness in their own lives and had a spark of inspiration: What if they could bring these practices into the classroom? What if they could give young people tools to manage stress, improve focus, and cultivate emotional well-being?

This idea wasn't born in a vacuum. It came at a time when concerns about youth mental health were growing. Stress, anxiety, and depression were on the rise among young people. Richard and Chris saw an opportunity to make a difference by offering a lifeline to students navigating the choppy waters of adolescence.

So, they rolled up their sleeves and got to work. They developed a curriculum called *".b"* (pronounced "dot-be"), which stands for *"Stop, Breathe, and Be."* It was designed to make mindfulness accessible and engaging for young people, using age-appropriate language, activities, and even a bit of humor.

Now, here's where the magic of mindfulness comes into play. The .b curriculum wasn't just about sitting still and breathing, although that's part of it. It was about helping students develop a kind of "inner toolkit." These would be tools to navigate difficult emotions, to improve concentration, to be kinder to themselves and others.

The results? They were nothing short of remarkable! Schools that implemented the program reported significant, positive changes. Students showed improved attention and focus. They were better able to manage stress and anxiety. Some even saw improvements in their academic performance.

But don't just take my word for it. Let's hear from some of the students themselves:

"It helps me to concentrate in class and to calm down when I'm stressed," says 14-year-old Rhonda.

"I use mindfulness before exams to help me relax and focus," shares 16-year-old James.

Teachers noticed changes, too. "The atmosphere in the classroom is calmer," reports Ms. Thompson, a high school English teacher. She added, *"Students seem more able to settle and engage with their work."*

The Mindfulness in Schools Project didn't stop with .b. They developed programs for younger children, for sixth form (ages 16-18 in the British education system), and even for school staff. The idea was to create a whole-school approach to mindfulness, fostering a culture of awareness and emotional intelligence.

Now, you might think, *"That's great for schools, but how does this apply to my life?"* Well, let's break it down:

Start Small: The MiSP shows us that even short, regular mindfulness practices have a big impact.

Make It Relevant: They adapted mindfulness techniques to suit their audiences. Think of a way that you can adapt mindfulness to fit your life and interests?

Create a Supportive Environment: The "whole school" approach reminds us that it's easier to maintain a practice when those around us are supportive.

Patience Pays Off: The benefits of mindfulness will increase over time. Trust the process.

Here's an exercise for you. This week, try adding a short mindfulness practice within your daily routine. It could be as simple as taking three mindful breaths before you start work, or you might deliberately focus on the sensation of washing your hands. Notice how these small moments of presence affect your day.

The Mindfulness in Schools Project reminds us that mindfulness isn't reserved for monks or yoga enthusiasts. It's a practical tool that can help us navigate the challenges of everyday life. And the earlier we start, the better equipped we will be to handle whatever life throws our way.

So, friends, as you continue on your mindfulness journey, remember the lessons from these innovative educators. Mindfulness is not about achieving a state of perpetual bliss. Instead, it's about developing the awareness and skills to meet life's difficulties with a bit more ease and a lot more kindness. What small step will you take today to bring more mindfulness into your world?

Mastering Mindfulness Challenges

Like any new habit, establishing a mindfulness practice can come with challenges. Here are some common ones, along with ways in which you could overcome them:

Dealing with Distractions: Your mind will wander during mindfulness practice, and that's okay. The practice is in noticing when your mind has wandered and gently bringing it back to the present moment.

Making Time for Mindfulness: Start small. Even five minutes a day makes a difference. You might find it helpful to link your practice to an existing habit, like practicing mindfulness right after you brush your teeth in the morning.

Handling Difficult Emotions: Sometimes, being present means facing uncomfortable feelings. Remember, the goal isn't to make these feelings go away, but to observe them without judgment. If things get too intense, it's okay to take a break or seek support from a mental health professional.

Stress Less: The Mindful Way

In our fast-paced world, stress has become a constant companion for many of us. But it doesn't have to be this way. Dr. Elizabeth Hoge,

Georgetown University Medical Center Psychiatrist, found that mindfulness meditation can help reduce anxiety symptoms in people with generalized anxiety disorder.

When you feel stressed, try this quick mindfulness exercise: Take five deep breaths, focusing your full attention on the sensation of the breath moving in and out of your body. This simple act will surely help activate your body's relaxation response, thereby reducing the effects of stress.

Focus Boost: Mindfulness at Work

Have you ever sat down to work on something important, only to find your mind wandering every few minutes? Mindfulness can help with that, too. Studies have found that mindfulness is able to enhance cognitive flexibility and improve working memory capacity.

Next time you need to focus, try this: Before starting your task, take a few mindful breaths. Set an intention to give the task your full attention. When you notice your mind wandering, gently bring it back to the task at hand, just as you would in a breathing meditation.

Mindful Connections

Practicing mindfulness can increase empathy and compassion, which leads to improved interpersonal relationships. When we're more aware of our own thoughts and feelings, we're better able to understand and relate to others.

Try bringing mindfulness into your next conversation. Really listen to the other person, noticing not only their words, but also their tone of voice and body language. Be aware of your own reactions without immediately acting upon them.

Sustaining Mindfulness: Long Term Strategies

Like any skill, mindfulness gets easier with practice. Allow me to offer some tips for creating a sustainable practice.

Set Realistic Goals: Start small and gradually increase your practice time.

Find a Mindfulness Community: Whether it's a local meditation group or an online forum, having a formal and steady support is guaranteed to help you stay motivated.

Use Technology to Support Your Practice: There are many great apps and online resources to guide you through mindfulness exercises.

As we conclude our exploration of mindfulness in daily life, let's take a moment to reflect on the transformative journey we've embarked upon. Remember that practicing mindfulness isn't about achieving perfection but cultivating awareness and presence in our everyday experiences. As Jon Kabat-Zinn, the founder of Mindfulness-Based Stress Reduction, wisely noted, *"The little things? The little moments? They aren't little."*

Throughout this chapter, we've delved deeply into the practice of mindfulness, uncovering its amazing impact upon our well-being and daily experiences. We've explored various techniques to bring mindfulness into our everyday lives, from formal meditation practices to informal moments of awareness.

This journey isn't limited to finding moments of calm; it's about transforming our relationship with ourselves and the world around us. And let's always remember the connection to the 3 C's Concept:

Compassion: Mindfulness enhances our awareness of others' emotions, fostering empathy and compassionate responses.

Creativity: By clearing mental clutter, mindfulness creates space for creative insights and innovative problem-solving.

Connection: Cultivating a mindful presence during our interactions deepens our connections with others and our environment.

REFLECTIONS - CHAPTER 7: MINDFULNESS MASTERY

Daily Mindfulness Assessment:

1. When did you feel most present today?
2. What distractions commonly pull you from the present moment?
3. How does your body feel during mindful moments?
4. Where do you notice mindfulness comes naturally?
5. What situations trigger automatic/unmindful reactions?

Weekly Mindfulness Tracker:

1. **Formal Practice Monitor** ▫ Morning meditation sessions ▫ Mindful breathing breaks ▫ Body scan practice ▫ Walking meditation Duration: _____ Quality (1-10): _____
2. **Informal Practice Log** ▫ Mindful eating moments ▫ Present-moment awareness ▫ Mindful conversations ▫ Mindful movement Frequency: _____ Ease (1-10): _____
3. **Awareness Checklist** ▫ Physical sensations noticed ▫ Emotional states observed ▫ Thought patterns recognized ▫ Environmental awareness Insights gained: _____

Implementation Tips:

- Start with 5-minute practices
- Use daily activities as mindfulness triggers
- Notice resistance without judgment
- Build gradually on small successes

REFLECTIONS - Chapter 7: Mindfulness Mastery

Your Mindfulness Journey

Mindfulness is the art of being fully present in each moment, observing your experience with curiosity and kindness. Use this space to explore your growing awareness and document your discoveries.

Journal Prompts:

- Describe a moment when you felt fully present
- What changes do you notice since beginning mindfulness practice?
- How does mindfulness affect your relationships?
- What surprises you about practicing mindfulness?

Exploring Your Experience:

- Notice any resistance to practice
- Record moments of clarity
- Document positive changes
- Note challenging situations

Space for Personal Observations:

Weekly Intention Setting: Choose one aspect of mindfulness to focus on this week:

Remember: Mindfulness is a practice of returning to the present moment again and again. Each time your mind wanders and you bring it back, you're building the muscle of awareness.

Key Insights from Chapter 7:

The greatest journey begins within...

EMBARK ON AN ODYSSEY

that will challenge everything you thought you knew

THE SAGA CONTINUES

DISCOVERING
YOUR LIFE'S
PURPOSE

Face the trials of self-doubt

BATTLE THE VILLAINS

of societal expectations

UNCOVER THE TREASURES

hidden in your passions and values

"A life-affirming quest!" • *"Deeply moving!"*
"A must-experience journey to your true calling!"

CHAPTER 8

Your destiny awaits...

DISCOVERING YOUR LIFE'S PURPOSE

*"The two most important days in your life are the day
you are born and the day you find out why."*
— Mark Twain

Why Purpose Matters

Everyone has moments when they ask themselves, "Why am I here?" This simple question is about finding your purpose. Now, what exactly is one's purpose? Having a purpose is like having a big goal. It is the thing that you feel you are meant to do, certainly more than a job or a hobby. When you wake up in the morning, it's having a purpose that makes you excited to start that day. So, finding your purpose makes you happy and feeling good inside.

Dr. Viktor Frankl, renowned Psychiatrist and Holocaust survivor, developed groundbreaking ideas about the importance of meaning in life. In his seminal work 'Man's Search for Meaning,' Frankl argued that the primary motivational force in humans is the search for meaning, even under the most extreme circumstances.

His observations in Nazi concentration camps showed that those who maintained a sense of purpose were more likely to survive and even thrive. Frankl's work is foundational to our understanding of purpose and its crucial role in human resilience and fulfillment.

Building on this, Dr. William Damon, a leading scholar of Human Development at *Stanford University*, has conducted extensive research on the role of purpose in life, especially among young people. His work suggests that having a purpose is not merely beneficial, but it is essential for thriving. Dr. Damon defines purpose as *"a stable and generalized intention to accomplish something that is at the same time meaningful to the self and consequential for the world beyond the self."*

In his landmark study, Damon found that only about 20% of youth have a clear sense of purpose. However, those who do are more likely to be highly engaged in school, show concern for their communities, and report higher levels of happiness and life satisfaction. This research highlights the importance of helping individuals, especially young people, to discover their purpose early in life.

Doing things that match your purpose feels like living the life you were meant to live. This feeling is potent. Having a purpose gives you a reason for your actions, and remembering your purpose will strengthen you during difficult times. It's like having a light inside you that never goes out and keeps you going.

This drive to do your best is called "resilience." Resilience is facing problems without giving up.

Having a purpose also gives you motivation. When your goal aligns with your purpose, you want to reach that goal very badly. You replace having to do something with *wanting* to do it. What a difference! It makes you work harder, feel proud of what you're doing, and possibly help others to find their purpose, too.

When you live a life with purpose, it's extraordinary. You are making your mark on the world while doing something that matters to you and others. So, finding your purpose is a big deal, I know! It changes how you see everything and what you actually determine to do every day.

Remember the stories I shared earlier about the compassionate lesson my grandfather taught me about financial responsibility? He wasn't just talking about money; he was showing me by example the power of purposeful teaching.

My father's creative approach to community policing through his "Officer Friendly" presentations showed me how a sense of purpose could bridge gaps and build trust among different groups of people. And that transformative moment when I heard Louis Armstrong play ignited a passion that would shape my career and my approach to connecting with others through music and storytelling.

These experiences, rooted in compassion, creativity, and connection, gradually coalesced into a sense of purpose that has guided my life's work. They taught me that purpose isn't always a single, clearly defined goal. Sometimes, it's a tapestry woven from the threads of our most meaningful experiences and the values they instill in us.

As you reflect on your own purpose, consider the moments in your life where you've felt most alive, most connected, or most impactful. These might be the signposts pointing toward your own unique purpose, just as my prior experiences pointed me toward a life dedicated to fostering compassion, creativity, and connection in others.

Ikigai: Your Reason for Being

Let's explore the Japanese concept of 'ikigai' (ee-key-guy), which means "reason for being." It's the "sweet spot" where four elements intersect: what you love, what you're good at, what the world needs, and what you can be paid for.

Take *Hiroshi Yamada*, a 72-year-old retiree from Tokyo. After years in a high-pressure job, retirement left him feeling lost and empty.

Remembering his grandmother's teachings about ikigai, Hiroshi set out to find his own reason for being at this stage in his life.

Hiroshi Yamada reflected on his passions of gardening and teaching, his skills of organization and patience, his community needs for green spaces and youth mentorships, and his potential income sources. The result? Hiroshi created a community garden, teaching kids about plants and sustainability. This project ticked all the boxes - he loved it, used his skills, met a community need, and earned a bit through plant sales and workshops.

Hiroshi's story shows how finding one's ikigai can lead to a profound sense of purpose and fulfillment, especially during major life transitions. As we continue exploring the role of purpose in a fulfilling life, consider your own ikigai:

- What activities bring you joy?
- What skills do you possess that others admire?
- What needs do you see in your community or the world?
- How might you align these elements to create a sense of purpose that resonates deeply with who you are?

Passion and Values Uncovered

Discovering what truly "makes us tick" is like finding a hidden treasure inside of us. It's about digging deeply to figure out what we love and what matters most to us. It is not a race; it's a journey that can make life exciting and meaningful. So, let's take it step by step.

Dr. Angela Duckworth's research on grit emphasizes the importance of passion in long-term success. She defines passion, not as fleeting excitement, but as a deep, enduring interest. Finding this kind of passion is crucial to identifying your purpose.

Take a moment right now to think about what you like to do. It could be something small like reading books or big like climbing mountains. Maybe you're into painting, dancing, or cooking. These are your passions. They are the activities that make you forget about time. When you're doing what you love, hours can pass like minutes. These activities give your life color and joy.

Now, let's talk about your values. Values are like a compass that guides you. They are the big ideas that you believe are valuable, like honesty, kindness, or courage. Your values steer you through life, consistently helping you decide between right and wrong. They can tell you when to say "yes" and when to stand up and say "no." Knowing your values is like having a secret weapon for making good choices.

So, how do we find out what our passions and values are? It starts with self-reflection. Self-reflection means taking time to ponder your life. Ask yourself: *"What have I always enjoyed doing? What activities make me feel strong and happy?"* Write these things down because they are clues to identifying your passions.

Next, think about times you felt proud of something you did. What was happening? What were you standing up for? Write these moments down, too. They tell you about your values.

Let's do more than think. Let's explore! Trying new things is a great way to find out what you love. You might find a new hobby or realize that helping others makes you feel great. Maybe you'll discover that you love learning new things. You know more about what distinguishes you from others when you try different activities.

Now, here's something interesting. Our passions and values often connect. If you love playing music and value creativity, you might find purpose in writing songs to share with the world. If you're passionate about sports and value teamwork, coaching a local kids' team might give you a sense of purpose. Finding where your passions and values meet is like finding your unique spot in the world.

Living with purpose naturally aligns with the 3 C's. A purposeful life often involves showing compassion, finding creative solutions to problems, and connecting deeply with others and our communities.

Purpose in Action: The TOMS Story

Imagine a business that changes lives with every product sold. Let's talk about a man who found his purpose and, in doing so, changed the lives of millions. This is the story of Blake Mycoskie, the founder of TOMS Shoes. It's a tale that shows us how compassion, creativity, and connection can come together to create something truly remarkable.

Blake's journey began in 2006 when he took a trip to Argentina. He wasn't looking to start a business; he was simply taking time off to volunteer and explore. But sometimes, purpose finds us when we least expect it.

During his travels, Blake noticed two things. First, he saw the hardships faced by children who didn't have shoes. These kids couldn't attend school, were at risk of disease, and faced daily challenges most of us can't imagine. Second, he observed the traditional Argentine Alpargata shoes—simple, comfortable, and practical.

Now, here's where the magic of the 3 C's comes into play. Blake felt a deep sense of compassion for these children. He connected with their struggles and the local community. And then his creativity kicked in. What if he could find a way to help these kids and create a sustainable business at the same time?

This moment of inspiration led to the birth of TOMS Shoes and its revolutionary "One for One" business model. For every pair of shoes sold, TOMS would give a pair to a child in need. It was compassion in action, creativity in business, and a powerful connection between consumers and those in need.

Blake's purpose became clear: to use business as a force for good. Yes, he was selling shoes. But more importantly, he was selling the chance to make a difference. And people resonated with this purpose. They knew that when they were buying this product, they were joining a movement.

But here's the thing about purpose—it's not always smooth sailing. Blake faced challenges. Some criticized the model, questioning its long-term impact. Others doubted the quality of the shoes. But Blake's sense of purpose kept him going. He listened to feedback, improved the product, and expanded the model.

TOMS evolved. They began producing eyewear, with each purchase providing sight to a person in need. They started a coffee line that helped provide clean water to developing communities. Blake's purpose grew and adapted, but the core remained the same, which was to improve lives through business.

Now, you might be thinking, *"That's great for Blake, but how does this apply to me?"* Well, let's break it down:

Compassion: Blake's journey started with empathy for others. What moves your heart? What injustices or challenges do you see that stir something inside you?

Creativity: Blake combined a traditional shoe design with an innovative business model. How can you creatively approach the challenges you see?

Connection: TOMS created a powerful connection between consumers and those in need. How can you foster meaningful connections in your life and work?

Purpose: Blake aligned his personal values with his business. Can you think of a concrete way that you might align your daily actions with what truly matters to you?

Remember, friends, finding your purpose isn't about grand gestures or changing the whole world overnight. No, it's about taking that first step, just like Blake did when he decided to create TOMS.

Here's an exercise you might like to try: Think about a problem you see in your community or the world. How could you apply compassion, creativity, and connection to address it, even in a small way? Write down your ideas. This could be the first step on your own purpose-driven journey.

Blake Mycoskie's story shows us that when we align our actions with our values, when we apply the 3 C's to our lives and work, we can create ripples of positive change that reach far beyond ourselves. Your purpose is out there, waiting for you to step into it. So, what will your next step be?

Purpose-Driven Goal Setting

Setting goals is like planning a road trip. You decide where you want to go. But not all trips are the same. Let's say you want to drive somewhere that makes you happy. This place is like your life's goal. It is a special place that feels right for you. It is important to choose goals that fit with who you are and what you care about. That's what makes the trip worthwhile, right?

Dr. Edwin Locke, a pioneer in Goal-setting Theory, found that specific and challenging goals lead to better performance than easy or vague goals. When these goals are aligned with our purpose, we're more likely to persist in pursuing them, even when we're faced with obstacles.

So, first think about what matters to you, what makes you get out of bed in the morning. Maybe it's helping people, creating something beautiful, or learning new things. These are clues to your purpose. Your purpose is like the fuel for your trip. It keeps you going, even when the road gets bumpy.

Once you know your purpose, you must set goals to match it. Goals that are tied to your purpose will feel right. They will be like signposts on your trip, pointing you in the right direction. And when you reach these goals, you will know that you are living the life that is right for you. That's a great feeling.

Let's talk about how to set these goals. You will want to be very clear about what you want to achieve, which means you must be specific. Instead of saying, *"I want to help people,"* you might say, *"I want to volunteer at a food bank weekly."* Set clear goals on which you can act upon.

After setting your goals, you need a plan to reach them. A plan is like a map for your road trip. It shows you the way to go. You might need to learn new skills or meet new people to help you. That's all part of the plan. And remember, it's okay to change your plan if you find a better way.

Your goals should also be realistic. It doesn't mean they should be easy, but they should be things you can accomplish. If you set a goal to become a famous singer, but you don't sing, that won't be a realistic goal. Pick goals you can work toward a little at a time. That way, you can keep moving forward.

It's also good to set goals for different parts of your life. Maybe you have goals each for your work, family, and hobbies. That's good. It's like making enough stops on your trip to eat, rest, and see exciting things.

When you work on your goals, keep your purpose in mind. Ask yourself, *"Is what I am doing helping me get to where I want to go?"* If the answer is "yes," then that's great! Keep going. If the answer is "no," then think about what you need to change. It's like checking your map to ensure you are still on the right road.

Talents with Purpose: Making an Impact

We all have something special inside of us. It's that thing we're naturally good at. Maybe you know what it is; perhaps you don't. But it's there. It's a talent or a skill that you have. And it's something you can use to help others. This section is about finding and using that talent to do good things in your town, school, or anywhere you can.

Dr. Martin Seligman, the "father" of Positive Psychology, introduced the concept of "signature strengths." These are our most prominent character traits and abilities. When we use these strengths in service of something greater than ourselves, we experience a sense of fulfillment and purpose.

As mentioned earlier, let's start with figuring out what you're good at. Think about what you love to do. These things that you love to do could be considered your talents. Knowing your skills is crucial. It's like knowing what tools you have in your toolbox. When you know what tools you have, you can use them to fix things, build things, or make things better.

Now, why is this important? When you use your talents to help others, don't you feel good? Don't you also make other people feel good? It's like giving someone a present and seeing them smile. And when you use your talents, you're giving the world a unique gift that only you can provide.

So, then, how do you use your talents to make a difference? Look around you. Some places and people need help. Maybe there's a park that needs cleaning up or an old neighbor who needs someone to talk to. You could draw pictures to make a friend smile if you like to draw. If you're good at singing, you could sing at a place where people are sick and cheer them up. You could help other kids with homework if you're good at math.

Every time you use your talents to help, you gradually improve your part of the world. It's like planting a seed that grows into a plant that makes everything look nicer. And just like a plant needs water to grow, your talents must also be used to grow. When you use your talents, you get better at demonstrating them. You learn more, and you do more. And the more you do, the more you are a help.

Doing good things with your talents also brings people together. When you help others, they feel happy and want to help someone else. It's like a chain reaction that creates a "pay it forward" scenario. One good thing leads to another, and soon, more people want to do good things, and ultimately, the world looks brighter.

Purpose Check: Realign and Refocus

Let's begin here by assuming that you've found your purpose, and you're living a life that feels right. That's fantastic! But here's the thing: life changes. You change. That's why it's crucial to regularly take a look at your life and ask, *"Is what I'm doing still in line with my purpose?"*

Developmental Psychologist Dr. Robert Kegan suggests that our understanding of our purpose can evolve as we grow and gain new experiences. He emphasizes the importance of periodically reassessing our goals and values to ensure that they still align with our evolving sense of self.

Things shift. What mattered to you last year might not be paramount to you today. And that's okay. It doesn't mean you've lost your way. It just means it's time to check in with yourself. It's like being a detective in your own life, looking for clues telling you whether you're on the path you want.

Reassessing your purpose isn't a one-time thing. It's ongoing. Look at it as an appointment with yourself. Maybe every few months or once a year, you sit down and think about your values and the steps you've taken in service of them. Are they moving you forward, or are they holding you back?

When you reassess, look at your actions. If they don't match your purpose, then realign. Slight adjustments can have significant impacts over time. Realignment ensures you keep moving in the right direction. Goals naturally shift, signaling a need to adjust your action plan. It's important to keep your goals fresh and exciting. They should light a fire in you, urging you forward.

An exercise to help you to realign with your purpose is to write down what you do each day for a few days. Then, next to each activity, write why you do it. This exercise reveals if your 'whys' are strong. If not, then you will want to find new ones.

Understand that reassessing and realigning with your purpose is not starting over. It's refining, honing in on what gives your life meaning. It's about staying true to who you are. And sometimes, staying true requires changing course.

When you make changes, do so with intention. Choose adjustments that feel right and that excite you. You're the author of your life, so you get to write your story. If a chapter isn't going how you like, you have the power to rewrite it.

Think of your sense of purpose as a compass. Even the most experienced sailors need to check their compass now and then to ensure they're going in the right direction. Your life is a voyage, and your purpose is your compass. Adjust your sails as needed and keep moving forward!

Community Service: A Path to Purpose

Let's explore how finding and living with purpose can transform lives and communities. Meet Miguel, a 35-year-old teacher who felt something was missing in his life despite his rewarding career. Miguel had always been passionate about education, but he felt he could do more for his community.

One day, while walking through his neighborhood, he noticed a group of kids playing on the street after school hours. He realized these children might benefit from additional learning opportunities and a safe space to spend their afternoons.

Inspired by this realization, Miguel decided to start an after-school program. He began by reaching out to his school administration and local community center for support. With their backing, he gathered a team of volunteer teachers and high school students to help run the program.

The after-school program offered homework help, reading sessions, and fun educational activities. Miguel faced many challenges, from securing funding to developing engaging curricula. But his sense of purpose kept him motivated.

As the program grew, Miguel saw its impact extend beyond academic improvement. The children were developing stronger social skills, gaining confidence, and showing more interest in their studies. Parents reported positive changes in their children's behavior at home.

Miguel's initiative also had a ripple effect in the community. Other teachers and community members were inspired to get involved, leading to the creation of additional programs like a community garden and a Neighborhood Watch group.

Through this journey, Miguel discovered that his purpose was more than teaching in a classroom. It included fostering a love for learning and creating opportunities for growth within his entire community. His story shows how purpose can evolve and expand, leading to meaningful change that touches many lives.

Never Too Late: Wally Funk's Purpose Journey

While we've talked about the importance of finding purpose early in life, it's never too late to discover or pursue your purpose. Let me tell you about Wally Funk, a woman who exemplifies this truth in an extraordinary way.

Wally Funk was born in 1939, and from a young age she had a passion for flying. In the 1960s, she was part of the "Mercury 13," a group of women who underwent the same rigorous testing as male astronauts but were ultimately denied the opportunity to go to space due to their gender. Despite this setback, Wally never gave up on her dream.

Throughout her life, Wally pursued her passion for aviation, becoming the first female air safety investigator for the *National Transportation Safety Board* and the first female civilian flight instructor at Fort Sill, Oklahoma. She continued to break barriers and inspire others in the field of aviation.

Wally's most incredible achievement came when she was 82 years old. In July 2021, she became the oldest to fly to space, joining Jeff Bezos on Blue Origin's first crewed spaceflight. This moment was the culmination of a lifelong dream and a powerful demonstration of the enduring nature of purpose.

Wally's story teaches us several important lessons about purpose:

Persistence Pays Off: Despite facing countless obstacles and waiting over 60 years, Wally never gave up on her dream of going to space.

Purpose Evolves: While Wally's core passion for flight remained constant, the method by which she pursued it changed over time. She found ways to live her purpose through various aviation-related roles.

It's Never Too Late: Wally's spaceflight at 82 proves that it's never too late to fulfill your purpose or pursue your dreams.

Purpose Drives Resilience: Wally's sense of purpose helped her overcome many setbacks and keep pushing forward.

Living Your Purpose Inspires Others: Wally's journey has inspired countless individuals, especially women and girls, who are interested in aviation and space exploration.

Wally Funk's story reminds us that purpose is not bound by age or circumstance. It's a driving force that can guide us throughout our lives, leading to fulfillment and inspiring others along the way.

Dr. Paul Farmer: A Purpose-Driven Life

As we conclude our exploration of purpose, let's look at a remarkable example of how finding and living one's purpose can transform, not only an individual's life, but also the lives of countless others touched by that individual.

Dr. Paul Farmer's story is one of unwavering commitment to a purpose that emerged early in his life and guided him until his last days. Born into an unconventional family that spent part of his childhood living in a bus, Farmer's exposure to poverty and hardship sparked a lifelong dedication to global health equity.

As a young man, Farmer visited Haiti and was deeply moved by the extreme poverty and lack of healthcare he witnessed. This experience crystallized his purpose: to provide high-quality healthcare to the world's poorest communities. Despite facing an uphill battle and skepticism from others who believed his goal was unrealistic, Farmer persisted.

In 1987, Farmer co-founded *Partners In Health* (*PIH*), an organization dedicated to bringing modern medical care to poor communities around the world. Starting with a small clinic in rural Haiti, *PIH* grew to serve millions of patients across multiple countries.

Farmer's purpose drove him to challenge conventional wisdom in global health. He believed that diseases of poverty could and should be treated with the same standard of care available in wealthy nations. This conviction led him to pioneer treatments for multi-drug-resistant tuberculosis in Peru and tackle the HIV/AIDS epidemic in Rwanda.

Throughout his career, Farmer balanced his medical practice with academia, becoming Professor at *Harvard Medical School* and writing influential books on global health. His work saved countless lives and inspired a generation of healthcare professionals to dedicate themselves to serving underserved communities.

Farmer's unwavering commitment to his purpose did come at a personal cost. He spent most of his time in the field, away from comforts and family. Yet, he found profound fulfillment in living true to his calling. He once said, *"The idea that some lives matter less is the root of all that is wrong with the world."*

Dr. Paul Farmer's life demonstrates the transformative power of purpose. By aligning his talents, passion, and actions with a clear sense of purpose, he not only found personal fulfillment but also changed the landscape of global health. His legacy continues to inspire others to find and pursue their own purpose with similar dedication.

Farmer's story reminds us that when we find our true purpose and commit to it wholeheartedly, we will realize accomplishments beyond our wildest dreams. It shows us that purpose is much more than personal satisfaction. It's about the impact we can have on the world around us.

As you reflect on your own purpose, I invite you to consider: What injustices move you to action? What problems do you feel compelled to solve? Where do your talents and the world's needs intersect? Your answers to these questions might just lead you to a purpose as profound and impactful as Dr. Paul Farmer's or Wally Funk's or Miguel's. You've got this!

As we conclude our exploration of "purpose," let's recap the transformative journey we've undertaken. Remember, finding and living our purpose isn't a one-time event, but an ongoing process that continually shapes and enriches our lives. As Psychiatrist Dr. Viktor Frankl observed, *"Those who have a 'why' to live, can bear with almost any 'how'."*

Throughout this chapter, we've delved deeply into the heart of purpose, uncovering its critical role in personal fulfillment and resilience. We've explored the intricate landscape of meaning-making, our values, passions, and the impact we wish to have on the world. This journey is truly one of self-discovery, and beyond this, it's about aligning our lives with what truly matters to us.

REFLECTIONS - CHAPTER 8: DISCOVERING YOUR LIFE'S PURPOSE

Purpose Discovery Assessment:

1. What activities bring you deep satisfaction?
2. When do you feel most useful to others?
3. What issues or causes move you to action?
4. Which of your talents serve others best?
5. What would you do if success was guaranteed?

Weekly Purpose Tracker:

1. **Meaning Monitor** □ Activities that felt purposeful □ Moments of deep fulfillment □ Impact on others □ Alignment with values
2. **Ikigai Elements** □ What you love doing □ What you're good at □ What the world needs □ What you can be paid for
3. **Purpose Indicators** □ Energy levels during tasks □ Sense of time passing □ Feeling of contribution □ Natural motivation

Implementation Tips:

- Notice what energizes vs. drains you
- Track when you lose track of time
- Document moments of fulfillment
- Record positive impact on others

REFLECTIONS - CHAPTER 8: DISCOVERING YOUR LIFE'S PURPOSE

Your Purpose Journey

Finding your purpose isn't about one grand revelation - it's about noticing the threads that weave meaning through your life. Use this space to explore the patterns and passions that point toward your unique contribution to the world.

Journal Prompts:

- What problems do you feel called to solve?
- Which accomplishments feel most meaningful?
- What legacy do you want to leave?
- Who inspires you and why?

Purpose Exploration:

- What did you love doing as a child?
- When do others naturally seek your help?
- What topics make you lose track of time?
- What would you do for free?

Space for Vision Development:

Weekly Purpose Practice: Choose one way to explore or express your purpose this week:

Remember: Your purpose often lies at the intersection of what you love, what you're good at, and what the world needs. Stay open to discovering it in unexpected places.

What clarity about your purpose emerged from Chapter 8?

COMING ATTRACTIONS

GET READY TO EXPERIENCE

"A self-care symphony that'll have you hitting replay on your life!"

THE SELF-CARE
REVOLUTION

FEATURING THE BREAKTHROUGH TRACKS

MINDFUL MORNING MELODY
"Start your day on the right note"

BOUNDARY-SETTING BLUES
"Your new anthem of self-respect"

EMOTIONAL WELLNESS WALTZ
"Dance your way to inner peace"

STREAMING IN CHAPTER 9

9

THE SELF-CARE REVOLUTION

"Self-care is not self-indulgence, it is self-preservation."
— Audre Lorde

Why Self-Care Matters

Self-care is like the fuel in our tank. Without it, we can't keep going. Think about what happens when a car runs out of gas. It stops working. In the same way, when we neglect taking care of ourselves, our health, comprised of our physical, emotional, and mental well-being, starts to suffer until we reach a point where we are non-functional.

Dr. Shauna Shapiro, a Clinical Psychologist and expert in mindfulness and self-compassion, emphasizes that self-care is not selfish but necessary for our overall well-being. Her research, published in the *Journal of Clinical Psychology*, demonstrates that mindfulness-based self-compassion practices do significantly reduce stress and anxiety while increasing overall life satisfaction.

Dr. Shapiro's work shows that individuals who engage in regular self-care through mindfulness and self-compassion are more resilient, have better mental health, and are more capable of caring for others. She promulgates the concept of "good enough" self-care, which focuses on consistency rather than perfection, making it more accessible and sustainable for everyone.

Our body is quite intelligent. It tells us when we need rest, eat food, or take a break. But more often than any of us would like to admit, we ignore these signs. We think we're too busy. We have jobs, homes to look after, and people who count on us. We can't stop, right? Wrong! We need to listen to our bodies. It's important.

When we don't care for ourselves, minor problems can turn into big ones. Our sleep might be affected. We could feel tired all day. Our mood might go up and down. We start forgetting things. Even our friends might notice that we're not ourselves.

And when we keep going without self-care, we inevitably get sick. We might catch colds often or feel pain in our bodies. These are signs from our body saying, *"Hey, I need some attention here!"*

But real self-care is about more than avoiding sickness. Taking care of ourselves helps us to do well in life. We think better, feel happier, and handle stress with a fair degree of confidence. Self-care makes us strong, like a tree that stands tall in a storm. It gives us the power to handle the harsh winds of life. Yes, friends, it's that important!

Your Self-Care Blueprint

It's like this. Put simply, you matter! Your health and happiness matter. That's why we need to discuss right here something vital -- your "Self-care Plan." This must be the one plan that fits you perfectly, like a key in a lock. It opens up the best parts of life for you. So, let's explore this, shall we?

Dr. Alex Korb, Neuroscientist and author, suggests that creating a personalized self-care plan will significantly reduce stress and improve overall well-being. He emphasizes the importance of tailoring self-care activities to individual preferences and needs.

First things first. We all are different. What works for one person might not work for another. That's why your Self-care Plan can't be a copy of someone else's. It's got to be made just for you. Think of it as a special recipe that has all your favorite ingredients. The goal is to make you feel good, stay healthy, and be happy.

However, before making this plan, we have to do some deep introspection. We need to check on different parts of your life. These are things like how your body feels and what makes your heart happy. We also think about the people we like to spend time with. Offering honest answers to these kinds of questions gives us the words that we will put into our plan.

Let's start with the body. The body needs things like exercise, good food, and sleep. Maybe you love taking walks or dancing in your room. Or perhaps you like eating apples and carrots. These are things you would put into your plan. And sleep, oh, sweet sleep, is so important. We need to make sure you get enough sleep to feel great, which means thinking hard about how we spend our time while depriving ourselves of sufficient sleep.

Next is the heart, the feelings. We all need time to relax and do things we love. Maybe for you, that's drawing or listening to music. Well, make sure your plan has plenty of this. It's like giving your heart a cozy blanket to snuggle with.

What about friends? People need people. Think about who makes you smile and feel safe. You need to make time to see these people with some degree of regularity, and when that's not possible, take advantage of the plethora of social media platforms to stay connected. Special people in your life are like sunshine on your face.

Now, we take all these things and write them down. We make a list or a chart. It says what you will do to care for your body, your emotions, and your friendships. This becomes your Self-care Plan. You can look at it daily and remember to do these good things for yourself.

Here's a simple template to get you started:

Physical Self-Care:

- Exercise (e.g., 30-minute walk 3 times a week)
- Nutrition (e.g., 5 servings of fruits and vegetables daily)
- Sleep: (e.g., 7-8 hours of sleep nightly)

Emotional Self-Care:

- Relaxation (e.g., 10 minutes of meditation daily)
- Hobbies (e.g., 1 hour working on a favorite hobby twice a week)

Social Self-Care:

- Connections (e.g., call a friend once a week, have dinner with family twice a week).

Now, realize that your plan can change. As life changes, your needs change too. That's okay. You can continually update your plan. It's always meant to fit you just right at each period in your growth and development.

If something doesn't work anymore, then find something that does work. It's like changing clothes for the weather. You wouldn't wear a snow jacket in the summer, would you?

Rest and Recharge: The Essentials

Let's talk about rest and how it's more than just sleeping. When we rest, our bodies repair themselves. And getting sufficient rest is surely more than something nice to do; it's a must for your total well-being.

To keep going each day, you need good rest. Think of it like charging a battery. If you don't charge it, it won't work. Simple, right?

Sleep Scientist and author, Dr. Matthew Walker, emphasizes the crucial role of sleep in our overall health and well-being. His research shows that adequate sleep improves memory, enhances creativity, and boosts the immune system.

First, take a look at your sleep, both the quality and the quantity of it. How's it going? Do you get enough? Sleep is when your body fixes itself and your brain takes a break. If you don't sleep well, you won't feel good. You might even get sick more often.

So, make sleep a big deal in your life. Go to bed at the same time every night, as often as possible. Make sure your room is dark and quiet. It helps your brain know that it's time to rest. Trust me, you'll start to feel better.

You might think, *"I don't have time to sleep more!"* But here's the thing. You won't do well during the day if you don't sleep well at night. You'll be tired and not able to think straight. So, in the end, you'll waste time. See what I mean? Getting enough sleep means you do better in less time. It's worth it to make the time.

Next, let's add in relaxation. Relaxation is not synonymous with being lazy. It's doing things that make you feel calm. It could be reading, drawing, or just sitting and thinking. Find things that help you "chill out."

Do them every day, even if it's just for a few minutes. It helps your brain take a break from stress, which I'm sure you'll agree is terrible for you. It can make you sick and feel sad, or worse, bring you to a point of despair. So, fighting stress with relaxation is a really big deal.

Here's a simple relaxation exercise you can try. I can personally attest to the fact that they work:

- Find a comfortable, quiet place to sit or lie down.

- Close your eyes and take a deep breath in through your nose, counting to four.
- Hold your breath for a count of four.
- Exhale slowly through your mouth, counting to four.
- Repeat this process four times.

This exercise, known as *"box breathing,"* will help you reduce stress and promote relaxation in just a few minutes.

Now, make your plan for rest. Write it down. What time will you go to sleep, except on rare occasions, and how much sleep time will you allow yourself to have? What will you do to relax? Having a plan makes it more likely you'll do it.

And after having a plan, discipline yourself to stick to your plan as best you can. Some days might be more challenging than others, which is fine. Just keep trying. Your body and brain will thank you.

Remember that taking care of yourself isn't selfish. It's smart. When you're rested and relaxed, you can do more for others. You're happier. You're better at your job. You're a better friend and family member. So, don't skip on rest. Make it a top thing in your life. Your future self will be glad you did.

Now, let's dive into a real-world example that brings our discussion of self-care to life. Sometimes, the most powerful lessons come from those who've learned them the hard way.

Enter Arianna Huffington, a woman whose journey from burnout to breakthrough beautifully illustrates the transformative power of prioritizing self-care.

Her story is a wake-up call (pun intended!) that reminds us why taking care of ourselves isn't a luxury but a necessity. So, grab a cozy blanket and settle in as we explore how one of the most influential women in media discovered the revolutionary power of rest.

Sleep Revolution -- Arianna's Wake Up Call

In the fast-paced world of media and technology, one woman's wake-up call became a movement. This is the story of Arianna Huffington and her Sleep Revolution. It's a tale that reminds us how sometimes the most powerful act of self-care is simply closing our eyes and getting some rest.

Let's say it's 2007, and Arianna Huffington is at the top of her game. She's running The Huffington Post, a groundbreaking online news platform. She's a recognized voice in media and politics. By all outward measures, she's successful. But success, as she was about to learn, came at a price.

One day, Arianna collapsed from exhaustion and lack of sleep. She hit her head on her desk, broke her cheekbone, and woke up in a pool of blood. It was a stark, painful reminder that something had to change. *"Is this what success looks like?"* she asked herself. This moment of crisis became the seed of a revolution—the Sleep Revolution.

Arianna realized that she, like so many of us, had bought into the myth that burnout is the price we must pay for success. She had been sacrificing sleep, thinking it would give her more time to work, more time to achieve.

But her serious fall, and the subsequent damage to her face, taught her the crucial lesson that without proper rest she was not really living. This is true for all of us who may be just surviving until we are forced to stop, like Arianna did.

After this "wake-up" call, she did something radical. She started prioritizing sleep, at first just for herself. She began advocating for the importance of sleep, challenging the *"sleep when you're dead"* mentality that pervades our culture. People listened to this credible character.

In 2016, Arianna published *The Sleep Revolution: Transforming Your Life, One Night at a Time*. The book was of course about her personal journey. Beyond that, it was an intense journey into the science of sleep, the history of our relationship with rest, and how our sleep-deprived culture harms our health, job performance, and relationships.

Arianna didn't stop at writing a book. She transformed her company's culture, installing nap rooms in the office and encouraging employees to disconnect from work after hours. She stepped down from her role at *The Huffington Post* to founded *Thrive Global*, a company dedicated to ending the stress and burnout epidemic.

The results were eye-opening. Employees reported feeling more productive, more creative, and happier. Arianna herself found she was making better decisions, had more energy, and was more present in her relationships.

Now, you might be thinking, *"That's great for Arianna, but how does this apply to me?"* Well, let's break it down:

Listen to Your Body: Arianna's wake-up call was dramatic, but our bodies often give us smaller signs that we need more rest. Are you listening?

Challenge Cultural Norms: Just because "everyone" is burning the candle at both ends doesn't mean it's healthy or productive.

Prioritize Rest: Sleep isn't a luxury or a sign of laziness. It's a biological necessity and a powerful tool for success.

Create Sleep-Friendly Environments: Whether at home or work, create spaces that support good sleep habits.

Here's an exercise for you that worked for me. This week, try going to bed thirty minutes earlier than usual. Keep a journal of how you feel during the day. Do you notice any changes in your mood, energy, or productivity?

Arianna Huffington's story reminds us that true self-care often means challenging our assumptions about what it takes to be successful.

It shows us that oftentimes, the most revolutionary act is simply getting a good night's sleep.

So, friends, as you continue on your journey of self-care, remember the lesson from Arianna's Sleep Revolution. In a world that often glorifies busyness and exhaustion, choosing rest is a powerful act of self-love and self-care.

What will you do tonight to revolutionize your sleep?

Boundary Setting: The Art of Saying No

We discussed the importance of setting boundaries in Chapter 4 when we talked about nurturing authentic relationships. Now, let's expand on this concept in the context of self-care, with a focus on how boundaries protect our energy and well-being.

Setting boundaries in self-care is like creating a protective bubble around our time and energy. It's about recognizing our limits and communicating them to others. This isn't just about saying "no" to others; it's about saying "yes" to yourself and your needs.

As we explored earlier with Dr. Brené Brown's insights on vulnerability, setting boundaries is another crucial aspect of authentic living. Expanding on her work, Dr. Brown reminds us that boundaries are a form of self-respect. She says, *"Daring to set boundaries is about having the courage to love ourselves, even when we risk disappointing others."* This aligns beautifully with our journey of self-discovery and growth through the 3 C's.

Just as we learned to embrace our values, we now learn to protect our well-being through setting and maintaining healthy boundaries. It's not about building walls to keep others out but about creating gates we can open or close as needed. This practice of boundary-setting is an act of self-compassion that allows us to show up more fully in our connections with others and in our creative endeavors.

Well, friends, setting boundaries is actually affirming that you matter and taking care of yourself and your needs matters, too. It's another way we honor our journey of growth and embody the principles of compassion, creativity, and connection in our daily lives.

In self-care, setting boundaries might look like:

Time Boundaries: Designating specific times for work, rest, and personal activities.

Emotional Boundaries: Choosing not to take on others' emotional burdens.

Physical Boundaries: Respecting our need for personal space and physical comfort.

Mental Boundaries: Protecting our headspace from negative influences or excessive information.

Remember…

> *Setting boundaries isn't about building walls; it's about creating healthy gates. It's okay to open these gates when you choose to, but it's equally okay to keep them closed when you need to recharge.*

Here's a new exercise to help you set self-care boundaries:

Identify Your Non-Negotiables: What are the self-care practices you absolutely need?

Communicate Clearly: Practice expressing your boundaries in a kind but firm manner.

Start Small: Begin with one or two boundaries and gradually increase.

Be Consistent: Stick to your boundaries, even when it's difficult.

It is incredibly important to remember that setting boundaries is an act of self-care in itself. It's about valuing yourself enough to protect your time, energy, and well-being from even well-intentioned individuals who nevertheless encroach upon your space.

Mindful Self-Care: Real-Life Success

Let's turn our attention to how engaging in purposeful self-care can make a profound difference, even for those facing significant personal challenges. Meet Joanne, a 32-year-old software developer who has been struggling with social anxiety for years.

Large gatherings left her feeling overwhelmed, and even small talk with colleagues could trigger intense feelings of discomfort. Joanne often found herself declining invitations and isolating herself, which only made her feel lonelier and more anxious.

One day, while reading about self-care, Joanne came to a startling realization. She had always thought of self-care as bubble baths and scented candles (nice!), but not particularly helpful for her anxiety. What if self-care could be more purposeful? What if it could be a tool to help her face her fears and build the life she wanted?

With this new perspective, Joanne decided to take a brave step. She researched local hobby groups and found a small knitting circle that met weekly at a nearby cafe. The thought of joining made her nervous, but she reminded herself that this was an act of self-care. She was caring for her need for connection and growth.

Joanne's first meeting with the knitting group was challenging. Her hands shook as she introduced herself, and she struggled to make eye contact.

However, the group was small and welcoming, and Joanne found comfort in focusing on the rhythmic motion of the knitting needles. She didn't have to make constant conversation—it was okay to sit quietly and knit.

As weeks passed, Joanne found herself looking forward to the meetings. The familiar faces and shared activity provided a sense of safety. Gradually, she felt more comfortable engaging in conversations. She learned that one of the group members also dealt with anxiety, and their shared experiences helped Joanne feel less alone.

Encouraged by her progress, Joanne started applying this purposeful self-care approach to other areas of her life. She began taking short walks during her lunch break, caring for both her physical health and her need for moments of calm during the workday. She started journaling before bed, a way to process her thoughts and emotions.

These acts of self-care didn't make Joanne's anxiety disappear overnight. There were still challenging days. But Joanne noticed that she had more tools to cope, more moments of joy in her day, and a growing sense of confidence. She was no longer just surviving—she was taking active steps toward thriving.

Navigating Self-Care Hurdles

While we've discussed the importance of self-care and how to implement it, it's also crucial to address some common challenges that you might face. Dr. Kristin Neff reminds us that self-care isn't always easy, and it's normal to encounter obstacles along the way.

One common challenge is feeling guilty about taking time for yourself. You might think, *"I have so much to do; I can't afford to relax."*

But remember, self-care isn't selfish. It's necessary. Think of it like putting on your own oxygen mask first on an airplane. You can't help others if you're not taking care of yourself.

Another challenge is consistency. It's easy to start a self-care routine, but it can be hard to maintain it. Dr. BJ Fogg, Stanford University Behavior Scientist, suggests starting with tiny habits.

For example, if you want to meditate daily, start with just one minute a day. It's so small that it's hard to skip, and over time, you can build on it.

You might also face external pressures that make self-care difficult. Maybe your work schedule is demanding, or family responsibilities leave you little time for yourself. In these cases, it's important to communicate your needs to others and find creative ways to incorporate self-care into your daily routine.

As I've said before, self-care looks different for everyone, and it may change as your life circumstances change. Be flexible and kind to yourself as you navigate these challenges.

Self-Care Impact: Measuring Success

It's important to track your progress and see how your self-care efforts are impacting your life. Doing this will help you maintain your Self-care Plan because you realize tangible results.

Here are some ways that I've been successful in measuring the effectiveness of my self-care routine:

Keep a Mood Journal: Rate your mood on a scale of 1-10 each day. Over time, you might notice improvements as you consistently practice self-care.

Track Your Energy Levels: Note how energetic you feel throughout the day. Self-care often leads to increased energy and vitality.

Monitor Your Stress Levels: Use a stress scale of 1-10 to track how stressed you feel each day, and you might even add the time of day where you feel the most stress. As you engage in self-care, you should see your stress levels decrease.

Observe Your Relationships: Are you finding it easier to connect with others? Are your interactions more positive? Good self-care is a great way to improve your relationships with others.

Notice Changes in Your Work or Productivity: Are you able to focus better? Are you more efficient? Self-care can often lead to improvements in these areas, as well.

Progress isn't always linear. There will always be ups and downs, but you always want to look for overall trends over time.

As we conclude our exploration of purposeful self-care, let's ruminate on the transformative journey we've embarked upon. We know that self-care isn't a luxury or an indulgence, but a vital practice that supports our ability to live out our purpose. As the poet Audre Lorde wisely observed, *"Self-care is not self-indulgence, it is self-preservation."*

Throughout this chapter, we've analyzed the heart of purposeful self-care, uncovering its critical role in our overall well-being and resilience. We've explored the multifaceted landscape of self-care, including the physical, emotional, and spiritual sides of us.

This journey was in no way a means to pamper us. Instead, the journey was our blueprint for creating a sturdy foundation from which we can reach for our dreams and live out our purpose more fully.

REFLECTIONS - CHAPTER 9: THE SELF-CARE REVOLUTION

Self-Care Assessment Questions:

1. How effectively are you meeting your basic needs?
2. Where do you most often sacrifice self-care?
3. What boundaries need strengthening?
4. How do you typically respond to stress?
5. What currently nurtures your well-being?

Weekly Self-Care Tracker:

1. **Physical Well-being Monitor** □ Sleep quality/hours □ Movement/exercise □ Nutrition choices □ Rest periods taken
2. **Emotional Care Check** □ Stress levels (1-10) □ Mood tracking □ Boundary maintenance □ Self-compassion moments
3. **Energy Management** □ Activities that energize □ Activities that drain □ Restorative practices used □ Balance achieved

Implementation Tips:

- Start with one small change
- Honor your limits
- Practice saying "no"
- Celebrate self-care wins

REFLECTIONS - CHAPTER 9: THE SELF-CARE REVOLUTION

Your Self-Care Journey

Self-care isn't selfish—it's essential for sustainable compassion, creativity, and connection. Use this space to explore your relationship with self-care and design practices that truly support your well-being.

Journal Prompts:

- When do you feel most nourished and why?
- What messages about self-care did you learn growing up?
- How does taking care of yourself impact your relationships?
- What would your ideal self-care routine look like?

Boundary Exploration:

- Where do you need stronger boundaries?
- What makes it hard to maintain boundaries?
- How can you better honor your needs?

Space for Personal Care Planning:

Weekly Intention: Choose one self-care practice to prioritize this week:

Remember: Self-care is a practice of self-respect and sustainability. Small, consistent actions build a foundation for lasting well-being.

Key Self-Care Insights from Chapter 9:

"MIND-BENDING!" *"REVOLUTIONARY!"* *"TRANSFORMATIVE!"*

IN A WORLD OF FIXED THINKING
COMES THE ULTIMATE AWAKENING

EMBRACING
THE GROWTH
MINDSET

"Once you see it, you can't unsee it"

EXPERIENCE THE IMPOSSIBLE:

CHALLENGES TRANSFORM
Into opportunities before your eyes

WITNESS LIMITATIONS
Shatter into infinite potential

DISCOVER THE TRUTH:
Your mind holds the key to everything

CHAPTER 10

PREPARE TO QUESTION EVERYTHING

EMBRACING THE GROWTH MINDSET

*"The mind is just like a muscle - the more you exercise it,
the stronger it gets and the more it can expand."*
— Idowu Koyenikan

Growth Mindset 101

Imagine your mind as a garden where thoughts and beliefs grow into success or doubt. A special kind of mindset called "growth mindset" can help you make significant, positive changes in your life. It's like magic soil that enables everything in the garden to grow better.

Dr. Carol Dweck introduced the concept of a growth mindset. Her groundbreaking work shows that people with a growth mindset believe their abilities can be developed through dedication and hard work. This view creates a love of learning and a resilience that is essential for great accomplishment.

A growth mindset is a way of thinking that says, *"I can get better."* It believes in change. It believes in learning. People with this mindset see everything as a chance to grow. They don't give up when things get tricky. They keep trying, and they learn from what didn't work. And then, they try again!

Learning to ride a bike exemplifies this: you fall, get up, keep trying, and eventually succeed. That's because you had a growth mindset. You didn't let the falls stop you. You used them to learn.

Conversely, a "fixed mindset" is like a garden patch that believes it can't grow. People with this mindset think, *"I can't change; I'm either good at something or not."* They feel stuck. If they try something that doesn't work, they think, *"I'm not good at this,"* and give up.

They don't see mistakes as chances to learn. They see them as signs of inherent inability. This way of thinking will likely shape your whole life. If you have a fixed mindset, you are not inclined to try new things, thereby missing out on all the fun and good stuff in life.

A growth mindset enables continuous improvement, learning, and finding new paths to happiness and success. It is a powerful tool for developing the 3 C's. It allows you and me to see challenges in showing compassion as opportunities for growth, to view creative setbacks as learning experiences, and to approach connections with openness and curiosity.

Dweck's Discovery: Growth in Schools

Let's talk about Dr. Carol Dweck's work in more detail. In classrooms across the world, a simple idea is transforming how students learn. This is the tale of Dr. Carol Dweck and her timely research on mindset. It's a journey that shows us how a simple shift in perspective unlocks potential and transforms lives.

Our story begins in the 1960s and 1970s when Carol Dweck, then a young researcher, became fascinated by how people cope with failure. She noticed something intriguing: some kids bounced back from setbacks, while others were devastated by even small failures. This observation sparked a question that would drive decades of research: "Why?"

As Dweck dug deeper, she uncovered an important truth: it wasn't the ability that made the difference, but the mindset. She identified two distinct mindsets: a fixed mindset, where people believe their existing qualities are carved in stone; and a growth mindset, where people believe their existing qualities can be enhanced through effort and learning.

This discovery was revolutionary! It suggested that changing how we think about our abilities would change our potential for growth and achievement. But Dweck didn't stop at proposing a theory. She wanted to see if this knowledge could make a real difference in people's lives.

Fast forward to 2007, in a seventh-grade classroom in East Harlem, New York. Dweck and her colleagues implemented a Mindset Intervention Program. They taught students about their brain's ability to form new connections and grow through effort and learning. The results were remarkable!

Students who learned about the growth mindset showed significant improvements in their math grades. But more than that, their whole attitude toward learning changed. They became more engaged, more resilient in the face of challenges, and more eager to take on difficult tasks.

One student, Maria, stood out. Before the intervention, she struggled with math and often said, *"I'm just not a math person."* After learning about the growth mindset, her perspective shifted. She started saying things like, *"I haven't figured it out yet, but I will if I keep trying."* Her grades improved, and her confidence and enthusiasm for learning soared.

The success in East Harlem was just the beginning. Schools across the country, and even around the world, began implementing growth mindset interventions. In California, a study of high school students showed that those who received a growth mindset intervention were more likely to take advanced math courses and perform better academically.

However, all of this wasn't only about academics. Athletes who adopted a growth mindset showed greater motivation with schoolwork and better performance in their chosen sport. Businesses that fostered a growth mindset culture saw increased employee engagement and innovation.

Now, you might be thinking, *"That's fascinating, but how does this apply to my life?"* Well, let's break it down:

Embrace Challenges: Instead of avoiding difficult tasks, see them as opportunities to grow your abilities.

Learn From Criticism: Rather than taking feedback personally, use it as valuable information to improve.

Find Lessons in Others' Success: Instead of feeling threatened by others' achievements, find inspiration and lessons in them.

Use the Power of "Yet": When you're struggling with something, add the word *"yet"* to your thoughts. *"I don't understand this... yet."*

Here's another exercise for you that I know for certain is helpful. This week, pay attention to your self-talk. When you face a challenge, notice if you're using fixed mindset language, such as, *"I can't do this,"* or growth mindset language such as, *"This is hard, but I can learn it."* Try to consciously shift to the growth mindset language and see how it affects your approach and outcomes.

Carol Dweck's research reminds us that our potential is not "set in stone." With the right mindset, we continually grow, learn, and achieve. It shows us that the power to change and improve is within our grasp, but it all starts with how we think.

So, friends, as you continue on your journey of personal growth, remember the lesson from Dweck's research. In a world that often tries to put limits on what we can achieve, adopting a growth mindset is a powerful act of self-belief and potential. How will you cultivate your growth mindset today?

Challenge Reframing: The Growth Way

When life throws a fast curveball at you, it's easy to feel knocked down. Maybe you wake up to a flat tire on a day packed with meetings. Or you spill coffee on your shirt right before an important presentation.

These moments can feel like a real test. But here's a thought: Could these setbacks be something else? Could they be opportunities in disguise?

Remember Dr. Angela Duckworth's insights on grit that we explored earlier? Her work sheds light on how we approach challenges. She suggests that individuals who view obstacles as chances to learn and improve are more likely to succeed in the long run. This perspective aligns beautifully with our discussion of the growth mindset.

Think about it. When something goes wrong, it's a chance to learn. It's not just an annoyance but an opportunity to practice solving problems quickly. When your tire is flat, you figure out who to call, how to get help, and how to make it to those meetings on time. And the coffee stain?

It's an opportunity to show that you can stay calm and carry on, even when things don't go as planned.

Yes, friends, I have another exercise to help you practice reframing:

- Think of a recent challenge you faced.
- Write down your initial thoughts about it.
- Now, try to write down three positive aspects or potential learning opportunities from this challenge.

- Reflect on how this new perspective changes your feelings about the situation.

Remember, reframing challenges as opportunities is a skill. And like any skill, it gets better with practice.

Self-Compassion: Failure's Friend

When we fail, our first reaction might be to get angry or upset with ourselves. We often think we should have done better. But there is another way to handle these challenging times. It's called self-compassion.

Revisiting Dr. Kristin Neff's work on self-compassion, which we explored earlier in our journey of self-discovery, we find its relevance extends to how we handle failure and challenges. Building on her definition of self-compassion, Neff's studies reveal that those who practice self-kindness are more resilient and demonstrate greater personal initiative and perceived competence. This underscores the importance of treating ourselves with understanding, especially when facing difficulties.

Self-compassion is when we treat ourselves with the same kindness as we exhibit for a good friend who has stumbled. When a friend fails, we don't scold them. Instead, we offer kind words and support. We tell them it's okay and that everyone makes mistakes. Extending this attitude to ourselves is what self-compassion is all about.

Allow me to offer a simple exercise to practice self-compassion:

- Think of a recent failure or mistake.
- Write down how you spoke to yourself about it.
- Now, imagine that a good friend made the same mistake, and write down what you would say to your good friend.
- Compare the two writings. How different are they?

- Practice speaking to yourself the way you would speak to a friend.

Self-compassion doesn't mean making excuses. It means acknowledging that everyone makes mistakes and that these mistakes are opportunities for growth.

Small Wins: Big Impact

Friends, have you ever thought about the small wins in your life? I mean, have you really thought about them? I'm not speaking about the big achievements, like getting a job or buying a house. No, I'm referring to the little things. Maybe you intentionally woke up early today or chose a salad over a burger. These things might seem tiny, but they're not. They are real wins, and they matter.

Dr. Teresa Amabile, Professor at Harvard Business School, has conducted extensive research on the power of progress. Her work reveals that of all the things that boost emotions, motivation, and perceptions during a workday, the single-most important thing is making progress in meaningful work.

Would you like to know a way to track and celebrate your small wins? I'm so glad you asked!

- Keep a "win" journal for three week, and at the end of each day, write down two small wins.
- At the end of each week reflect upon how these small wins contributed to helping you reach your larger goals.
- Choose one win to celebrate each week. You might treat yourself to your favorite coffee or take an extra-long bath, or even buy that something you've wanted.

Every step forward, no matter how small, is progress. And progress is worth celebrating.

Feedback: Fuel for Growth

Feedback is a gift. It's like getting the secret code to a game. It helps you play better. When someone whom you trust offers you advice, you're getting a tool to improve, so accept it and use it well.

Dr. Adam Grant, Organizational Psychologist, emphasizes the importance of seeking feedback for personal and professional growth. His research demonstrates that individuals who actively seek feedback perform better and are more likely to be promoted than those who don't.

Here's how you can make seeking feedback a regular practice:

- Identify three people whose opinions you value.
- Ask them for specific feedback on an area in which you're trying to improve.
- Listen completely without thinking of defending yourself. You can take notes if it helps.
- Thank them for their input, even if it's hard to hear.
- Reflect on the feedback and identify one action you can take, based upon what you gleaned.

Remind yourself that the goal isn't to please everyone or to change who you are fundamentally. It's to gather information that can help you grow and improve.

Deliberate Practice: Mastery's Secret

Now, let's talk about getting really good at something. I mean, expert-level good! Psychologist Dr. Anders Ericsson, who studied expert performance for decades, found that mastering something is not just about putting in time. It's about how you practice. He called it "deliberate practice."

Deliberate practice involves more than repeating something over and over. It's about pushing yourself just beyond your comfort zone, getting immediate feedback, and then using that feedback to improve. It's like having a personal trainer for whatever skill you're trying to develop. We embrace the concept of purposeful practice in sports and maybe arts, but now we see its potential within our lives.

Here's how you can apply deliberate practice to your own growth:

Set specific goals. Don't just say, *"I want to get better at public speaking."* Say instead, *"I want to improve my ability to use storytelling in my presentations."*

Break the skill down into components. For public speaking, this might include voice projection, body language, and content structure.

Get out of your comfort zone. If you're comfortable speaking to groups of 10, try speaking to a group of 20.

Seek immediate feedback. Record yourself, ask for audience feedback, or work with a coach to get the maximum constructive criticism you need.

Reflect and adjust. Use the feedback to focus on specific areas for improvement in your next practice session.

Remember, deliberate practice isn't always fun. It will certainly be challenging and sometimes frustrating. But it's the fastest way to improve any skill, and you'll see that it's worth the effort.

Growth Mindset: Life-Wide Application

A growth mindset isn't only thought about for school or work. It can transform every area of your life. Let me suggest some areas where you can apply it in different contexts:

Relationships: Instead of thinking, *"We're just not compatible,"* try saying, *"We can learn to communicate better."*

Health and Fitness: Replace *"I'm not athletic"* with *"I can improve my fitness with consistent effort."*

Creative Pursuits: Shift from telling yourself, *"I'm not artistic,"* to *"I can develop my artistic skills through practice."*

Personal Finance: Instead of expressing to others, *"I'm bad with money,"* think, *"I can learn to manage my finances more effectively."*

In each of these areas, look for opportunities to learn and grow. Embrace any challenges as chances to improve. Feel comfort in knowing that every expert was once a beginner.

Mindset Interventions: Proven Impact

Dr. David Yeager, University of Texas at Austin Psychologist, has conducted innovative research on the impact of growth mindset interventions, particularly in education. His studies have shown that even brief interventions when teaching students about the malleability of intelligence can significantly improve their academic performance.

In one study, Yeager and his colleagues found that a low-cost, scalable growth mindset intervention improved grades among lower-achieving students and increased overall enrollment in advanced mathematics courses. This research shows that fostering a growth mindset can have real, measurable effects on student outcomes.

What's particularly exciting about Yeager's work is that it shows how relatively minor changes in mindset can lead to substantial real-world impacts. This isn't just about feeling good — it's about concrete improvements in performance and life outcomes.

Growth Mindset Heroes

Let's look at some real-life examples of people who've embraced a growth mindset, as I share some of their positive experiences.

J.K. Rowling: Before *Harry Potter* became a global phenomenon, Rowling faced numerous rejections. She was a single mother living on welfare when she wrote the first *Harry Potter* book. Publishers rejected her manuscript multiple times, but Rowling didn't give up. She viewed each rejection as feedback rather than failure, using it to refine her work. Her perseverance and growth mindset ultimately led to the creation of one of the most successful book series in history.

Michael Jordan: Many people know Michael Jordan as one of the greatest basketball players of all time, but his journey wasn't always smooth. Jordan was actually cut from his high school basketball team. Instead of accepting this as a final verdict on his abilities, he used it as motivation. Jordan said, *"I have failed over and over and over again in my life. And that is why I succeed."* He practiced relentlessly, often staying after team practice to work on his skills. His growth mindset led him to become not just a team member, but a basketball legend.

Thomas Edison: Thomas Edison's journey to inventing the light bulb is a classic example of the growth mindset in action. He didn't succeed on his first try or his hundredth. In fact, it reportedly took him 1,000 attempts to successfully create the light bulb. When a reporter asked him how it felt to fail 1,000 times, Edison famously replied, *"I didn't fail 1,000 times. The light bulb was an invention with 1,000 steps."* This perspective epitomizes the growth mindset approach to challenges. Edison saw each "failure" as a necessary step toward success, not as a reflection of his lack of abilities.

Malala Yousafzai: The Pakistani activist for female education demonstrates an incredible growth mindset in the face of extreme adversity. Despite being shot by the Taliban for her advocacy, Malala continued to fight for education rights. She didn't view the attempt on her life as a reason to give up, but rather as motivation to spread her message even further. Her unwavering commitment and resilience in the face of adversity highlight the strength of a growth mindset. Malala's story teaches us that with determination and a belief in our ability to grow and make a difference, we can overcome even the most daunting obstacles.

Nate, the Adaptive Climber: Consider Nate, a 28-year-old graphic designer who has always been passionate about rock climbing. Three years ago, Nate was in a car accident that left him with limited mobility in his left arm. At first, Nate thought his climbing days were over. But instead of giving up, Nate embraced a growth mindset. He researched adaptive climbing techniques, worked with a physical therapist, and developed a unique climbing style that worked for him. Nate's story shows us that with creativity, perseverance, and a growth mindset, it's possible to adapt and thrive in the face of adversity.

These five stories remind us that a growth mindset is not just about achieving personal success, but also about persevering in the face of adversity to make a positive impact on the world. By embracing challenges and learning from failures, we can achieve our goals and inspire others to do the same.

As we conclude our exploration of the growth mindset, let's re-visit the transformative journey we've undertaken. Developing a growth mindset isn't a one-time achievement. It's an ongoing process that continually shapes our approach to life's challenges and opportunities. As Carol Dweck, the pioneering researcher in this field, wisely noted, *"Becoming is better than being."*

Throughout this chapter, we've delved deeply into the power of the growth mindset, uncovering its critical role in personal development and achievement. We've explored how our beliefs about our abilities does profoundly impact our success, resilience, and overall well-being.

This journey takes us beyond changing our thoughts because we've learned how to rewire our brains for lifelong learning and growth.

REFLECTIONS - CHAPTER 10: EMBRACING THE GROWTH MINDSET

Growth Mindset Assessment:

1. How do you typically respond to challenges?
2. When do you find yourself using fixed mindset language?
3. How do you handle mistakes and failures?
4. What triggers your self-limiting beliefs?
5. Where have you seen growth through effort?

Weekly Mindset Tracker:

1. **Challenge Response Monitor** ▫ Document challenges faced ▫ Record initial reactions ▫ Note mindset shifts ▫ Track growth opportunities taken/avoided
2. **Language Pattern Observer** ▫ "Yet" statements used ▫ Fixed mindset phrases caught ▫ Growth-oriented self-talk ▫ Limiting belief challenges
3. **Learning Experience Log** ▫ New skills attempted ▫ Comfort zone stretches ▫ Feedback received/applied ▫ Progress celebrated

Implementation Tips:

- Catch fixed mindset thoughts
- Add "yet" to limiting statements
- Celebrate effort over outcome
- View challenges as opportunities

REFLECTIONS - Chapter 10: Embracing the Growth Mindset

Your Growth Journey

The shift from fixed to growth mindset happens one thought, one choice, one moment at a time. Use this space to explore your mindset evolution and celebrate your growing capacity for change.

Journal Prompts:

- Describe a recent "growth moment" where you pushed past limitations
- What would you try if you knew you couldn't fail?
- How has your view of challenges changed since starting this chapter?
- What new possibilities are opening up as your mindset shifts?

Growth Reflection Questions:

- Where do you see evidence of your ability to grow?
- What fixed mindset beliefs are you ready to challenge?
- How could embracing growth change your relationships?

Space for Transformation Notes:

Weekly Growth Intention: Choose one area to apply the growth mindset this week:

Remember: Every challenge is an opportunity to grow. Your abilities aren't fixed - they're waiting to be developed through dedication and effort.

What growth opportunities emerged from Chapter 10?

WHEN LIFE PUSHES BACK...
YOU PUSH HARDER

STAND STRONG!

BUILDING UNSHAKEABLE RESILIENCE

From adversity comes strength...

WITNESS THE TRIUMPH OF THE HUMAN SPIRIT

HEART-POUNDING RESILIENCE
"Face every storm and emerge stronger!"

SOARING MELODIES OF HOPE
"Rise above life's challenges!"

UNBREAKABLE SPIRIT
"Nothing can hold you down!"

CHAPTER 11

GET READY TO BOUNCE BACK STRONGER!

11

BUILDING UNSHAKEABLE RESILIENCE

"I can be changed by what happens to me.
But I refuse to be reduced by it."
— Maya Angelou

Resilience. It's a word that brings to mind the image of a strong tree standing tall in the face of a raging storm. But resilience is not just about withstanding the storm. Resilience is bouncing back even stronger after the storm. It's facing life's challenges head-on and coming out on the other side unscathed, but also improved. So, why does resilience matter?

Dr. Ann Masten, a pioneering researcher in resilience, describes it as *"the capacity of a dynamic system to adapt successfully to disturbances that threaten its function, viability, or development."* In simpler terms, it's our ability to bounce back from adversity and grow from our experiences.

When life throws a curveball, it can be tough, really tough. We might face a problem at work, a challenge in our personal lives, or an unexpected event that shakes us to our core. In these moments, resilience helps us stand up and keep moving forward. It's crucial because there are times when a setback knocks us down with the intent to keep us down. But when we possess resilience, we rise, we learn, and we overcome.

Resilience Building Blocks

Let's break down the building blocks of resilience. Think of resilience as a house. To make that house sturdy, we need solid materials. In the world of resilience, these materials are factors like self-awareness, social support, and problem-solving skills. These aren't just ideas, but they are actually the concrete and steel of our resilience house.

Researchers Dr. Karen Reivich and Dr. Andrew Shatté have identified several key components of resilience:

- Self-awareness
- Emotion regulation
- Optimism
- Flexible thinking
- Strong relationships
- Self-efficacy
- Willingness to take on challenges

Self-awareness is knowing who you are and how you think. It's looking in the mirror and liking the person staring back at you. It's knowing your strengths, your weaknesses, and your limits.

When you're self-aware, you can tell when you're stressed and need a break. You recognize when a challenge is an opportunity to grow, rather than merely a problem to avoid.

Social support is just as important. Think of it as the friendly neighbor who comes over to help you put up the drywall in your resilience house. These friends, family, and colleagues are there for you when you need them. They're the ones who listen, encourage, and offer a helping hand or a kind word when the going gets tough. They remind you that you're not alone.

Reframing: The Resilience Lens

Life throws curveballs. Things go wrong. We all face tough times. What is the key to getting through these rough patches? It's Reframing. Let's talk about what that means and how you can do it.

As we've explored earlier in **Chapter 10**, Dr. Carol Dweck's work on growth mindset has far-reaching implications. Building on her insights, we see how this concept applies to resilience. She explains that our view of challenges significantly impacts our ability to recover from them.

Those with a growth mindset who believe their abilities can be developed are the people who see challenges as opportunities to learn and grow, rather than to see them as threats to their personal security. This perspective enhances resilience, allowing individuals to face adversity with a more adaptive mindset.

The first thing to understand about reframing is that we don't pretend everything's okay when it's not. No, reframing is about looking at the same situation differently and finding a new angle. Let's say you didn't get the job you wanted. Instead of thinking, *"I failed,"* try thinking, *"I learned from this experience how to do better next time."*

Why is this important? Because our thoughts have the power to change our feelings. When we think more positively, we feel better, too. And feeling better helps us bounce back. It's a big part of being resilient.

So, how does one reframe? Start by catching your negative thoughts. Notice when you find yourself thinking something negative. Pause and ask yourself, *"Is there another way to see this?"* Look for the learning. Look for growth. It's there, I promise, even in the hardest of situations. I like to call this the art of turning a frown upside down.

You know, friends, that I have had much experience reframing difficult situations in my life. So, here's an exercise to help you practice reframing:

- Think of a recent challenge you faced.
- Write down your initial thoughts about it.
- Now, try to write down three positive aspects or potential learning opportunities from this challenge.
- Reflect on how this new perspective changes your feelings about the situation.

Remember, reframing challenges as opportunities is a skill. And like any skill, it gets better with practice.

Coping Toolkit: Stress-Busting Strategies

Everyone would agree that life is full of difficulties. Stress and hard times are part of the journey. But you don't have to let them beat you. You can learn to cope, handle stress, and take back your peace in the midst of hard times. The key is having the right tools.

Dr. Susan Folkman and Dr. Richard Lazarus, pioneers in coping research, define coping as *"constantly changing cognitive and behavioral efforts to manage specific external and/or internal demands that are appraised as taxing or exceeding the resources of the person."*

Here are some effective coping strategies:

Deep Breathing: A simple technique that can calm your mind and body.

Mindfulness Meditation: Helps you stay present and reduce stress.

Physical Exercise: Releases endorphins and improves **your** mood.

Journaling: Allows you to process your thoughts and emotions.

Seeking Social Support: Talking to friends or family can provide comfort and new perspectives.

We must remember that different strategies work for different people and situations. Therefore, it's important to develop a diverse toolkit of coping strategies you can draw from as needed.

Support Network: Your Resilience Team

Getting by with a little help from our friends isn't just a catchy line from a beloved song. It's essential to our well-being and resilience. Dr. Emmy Werner, in her landmark study on resilience, found that resilient individuals were more likely to have strong social support networks.

Now, you might be wondering what a support network looks like. It could involve your family or your best buddies. It can also be anyone who gives you good vibes. It might be a friendly neighbor, a caring co-worker, or even a kind person with whom you chat at the coffee shop. These people make you smile and help you feel strong inside. And guess what? You can be that person for others, too. Pretty cool, right?

Building this network isn't as complicated as it sounds. You start small. Say "hello" to that neighbor. Share a joke with a co-worker. Make time for coffee with a friend. Listen when they talk, without you having any mind distractions. Offer a hand if they need it. It's about giving and taking. You're there for them, and they're there for you. It's a team effort.

I offer an exercise to help you practice: This week, challenge yourself to have three brief conversations with people you don't know well. It could be a neighbor, a colleague you rarely talk to, or even the barista at your local coffee shop.

After each conversation, jot down one thing you learned about that person. At the end of the week, reflect on these interactions. How did they make you feel? Did you discover any surprising commonalities?

Remember, every friendship starts small. One talk. One laugh. One shared thing. Then, it grows like a plant. It needs time and care. But soon it can be big and strong, full of laughs and talks and shared days in the company of others.

Self-Compassion: Resilience's Best Friend

When we fail, our first reaction might be to get angry or upset with ourselves. We often think we should have done better. But there is another way to handle these challenging times. It's called self-compassion.

Dr. Amit Sood, Professor of Medicine at the Mayo Clinic, and an expert in stress management and resilience, offers a thoughtful perspective on self-compassion within the context of resilience. His research, outlined in his book *The Mayo Clinic Guide to Stress-Free Living*, introduces the concept of "smart compassion." Dr. Sood argues that resilience is built through a combination of self-compassion and pragmatic action.

According to Dr. Sood, smart compassion involves acknowledging our struggles without becoming overwhelmed by them. It's treating each of us with kindness while also maintaining a sense of agency and purpose.

His studies reveal that individuals who practice smart compassion demonstrate greater emotional resilience, plus improved stress management, and finally enhanced overall well-being.

Dr. Sood's approach emphasizes the importance of training our attention to focus on gratitude and compassion, which he believes are key components of resilience. He proposes specific exercises, such as the "morning gratitude practice" and the "two-minute reset," which can help cultivate resilience in our daily lives.

Here's a simple exercise to practice smart compassion, based on Dr. Sood's work:

- Think of a recent challenge or failure.
- Acknowledge your feelings about this situation without judgment.
- Identify one thing you're grateful for despite this challenge.

- Consider one small, practical step you can take to address the situation.
- Offer yourself words of encouragement, as you would to a friend facing a similar situation.

This exercise combines self-kindness with practical action, embodying the principle of smart compassion.

But be careful not to assume that self-compassion means making excuses. It means acknowledging that everyone makes mistakes and that these mistakes are opportunities for growth.

Change Mastery: Thriving in Uncertainty

Change is a big deal that happens all the time. Change is natural. The challenge is not getting stuck. And it can be scary, right? But let's slow down and talk about why change is good. Change means something new is happening. It means we get to try things we haven't tried before. And that's where we can learn a lot.

When something changes, it's like getting a surprise. Sometimes, surprises are fun. Sometimes, they are not what we want. But either way, we definitely learn from them. Change helps us grow. It makes us stronger and wiser.

Now, let's talk about how to be okay with change. First, we should try to see good things that might come from change. Instead of thinking, *"Oh no, this is bad,"* we can intentionally say, *"What can I learn from this, and how can it help me?"* This way of thinking is called having a "positive outlook." Put another way, it means looking for the good while recognizing the bad.

We can also make a habit of learning new things. When we learn, we're changing a little bit. And that's good practice for when monumental changes happen. Try picking up a new book or learning a new game. It's fun and good for our brains.

In the end, change and uncertainty are parts of life. But we have the tools to work with them. We can keep a positive outlook, plan, hold onto what we know, talk to our friends and family, and learn new things. All these will help us feel strong and ready for whatever comes next.

Resilience in Action: Real-Life Heroes

Resilience is the ability to bounce back from adversity, and few individuals exemplify this quality better than Nelson Mandela and Oprah Winfrey.

Nelson Mandela, the former South African President, spent twenty-seven years in prison for his fight against Apartheid. Despite the harsh conditions and the long years of confinement, Mandela emerged with a spirit of forgiveness and a vision for a united South Africa. His resilience not only helped him survive almost three decades of his life, but it also enabled him to lead his country toward reconciliation and peace. Mandela's story teaches us that resilience is much more than enduring hardships. Resilience is also maintaining hope and working toward a greater good.

Oprah Winfrey, the media mogul, faced many challenges in her early life, including poverty, abuse, and discrimination. However, she used these experiences to fuel her determination and drive. Through resilience and hard work, Oprah built a media empire and became one of the most influential figures in the world. Her journey shows us how often her resilience transformed adversity into opportunities for growth and success.

These examples remind us that resilience is a powerful force to help us overcome obstacles and achieve our goals. By learning from the stories of two influential, public figures, we can find the strength to face our own challenges with courage and determination.

As we conclude our exploration of resilience, let's reflect on the transformative journey we've undertaken. Remember, building resilience isn't about becoming invulnerable, but about developing the strength to bounce back from adversity and grow stronger through our challenges. Psychiatrist Dr. Viktor Frankl observed, *"When we are no longer able to change a situation, we are challenged to change ourselves."*

Throughout this chapter, we've discussed in detail the foundations of resilience, uncovering its critical role in personal growth and well-being. We've explored the building blocks of resilience -- from self-awareness and emotion regulation to optimism and strong relationships.

This journey isn't just about surviving tough times; it's about thriving in the face of adversity and emerging stronger on the other side.

REFLECTIONS - CHAPTER 11: BUILDING UNSHAKEABLE RESILIENCE

Resilience Assessment Questions:

1. How do you typically respond to setbacks?
2. What helps you bounce back from difficulties?
3. Which coping strategies work best for you?
4. Where do you find strength during challenges?
5. Who supports you through tough times?

Weekly Resilience Tracker:

1. **Challenge Response Monitor** □ Document daily challenges faced □ Record initial reactions □ Track coping strategies used □ Note recovery time □ Rate effectiveness (1-10)
2. **Strength Building Practice** □ Self-care actions taken □ Support system engagement □ Boundary setting moments □ Positive self-talk instances □ New skills developed
3. **Growth Through Adversity** □ Lessons learned from difficulties □ Adaptations made □ Resources discovered □ Progress observed □ Victories celebrated

Implementation Tips:

- Start with small challenges
- Build your support network
- Practice preventive self-care
- Document what works
- Celebrate small wins

REFLECTIONS - CHAPTER 11: BUILDING UNSHAKEABLE RESILIENCE

Your Resilience Journey

Resilience isn't about never falling - it's about rising stronger each time. Use this space to explore your growing capacity to face life's challenges with grace and strength.

Journal Prompts:

- Describe a time you showed unexpected strength
- What helps you maintain hope during difficulties?
- Who or what inspires your resilience?
- How has adversity shaped who you are?

Resilience Resources: List your current tools for bouncing back:

1. **Internal Resources** (strengths, beliefs, attitudes):

1. **External Resources** (people, places, activities):

Space for Personal Growth Notes:

Weekly Resilience Focus: Choose one area to strengthen this week:

Remember: Resilience grows through practice and patience. Each challenge you face is an opportunity to build your capacity for bouncing back stronger.

What insights about resilience resonated most from Chapter 11?

COMING ATTRACTIONS

THE CLIMACTIC EVENT
11 EPISODES HAVE LED TO THIS

DON'T MISS IT!

LIVING
THE
3 C's

Where Theory Meets Practice

FEATURING THE SHOWSTOPPING

COMPASSION REVELATION

CREATIVITY BREAKTHROUGH

CONNECTION MASTERY

"REVOLUTIONARY" • *"LIFE-CHANGING"* • *"UNMISSABLE"*

A PIVOTAL MOMENT
CHAPTER 12
Get ready for the transformation

LIVING THE 3 C'S

"A journey of a thousand miles begins with a single step."
— Lao Tzu

As we've explored throughout this book, compassion, creativity, and connection are not isolated concepts—they're interwoven aspects of a fulfilling life. This chapter will explore how to consciously integrate these three powerful forces into our daily lives.

3 C's Alignment: Daily Practice

So, you have this idea. It's about living your life in a way that feels right. It's about being kind, connecting with people, and creating new things. How do you know if you're living by the 3 C's: compassion, connection, and creativity?

It's simple, and yet it's big. You look at what you do every day. Do the things that you do, based upon the choices that you make give thought to these 3 C's? If "yes," then great. If not, don't worry. There's a way to make it better.

Remember Dr. Sonja Lyubomirsky's research on kindness that I discussed earlier? Her work goes even deeper. As the distinguished Professor of Psychology and author of *The How of Happiness*, she offers valuable insights that align beautifully with our 3 C's.

Her research contains a fascinating breakdown of happiness: 50% is determined by genetics, 10% by life circumstances, and a whopping 40% by our intentional activities and practices. This means that, just like doing those acts of kindness, we have significant power to influence our own happiness through the choices we make and the practices we adopt. It's like we're the architects of much of our own joy!

Lyubomirsky's work suggests that deliberately cultivating positive behaviors and mindsets, such as those embodied in compassion, creativity, and connection, substantially increase our overall well-being. Her studies show that engaging in acts of kindness (compassion), pursuing meaningful goals (creativity), and nurturing social relationships (connection) are among the most effective strategies for enhancing happiness and life satisfaction.

Particularly relevant to our discussion of integrating the 3 C's, Lyubomirsky's research emphasizes the importance of variety and intentionality in well-being practices. She found that people who engaged in a variety of happiness-boosting activities, rather than repeating the same ones, showed greater increases in well-being. This underscores the value of approaching the 3 C's from multiple angles and consistently finding new ways to embody them in our lives.

To apply Dr. Lyubomirsky's conclusions to your journey with the 3 C's, I invite you to consider the following strategies:

- Practice gratitude regularly but in varying ways (e.g., journaling, verbal expressions, acts of appreciation).

- Engage in acts of kindness, alternating between planned and spontaneous gestures.
- Nurture relationships through different means (e.g., deep conversations, shared activities, supportive actions).
- Set and pursue meaningful goals that challenge your creativity in diverse areas of your life.
- Reflect on and savor positive experiences related to compassion, creativity, and connection.

By incorporating even some of these evidence-based practices into your daily life, you you will notice that you have enhanced the integration of the 3 C's within your daily living and boosted your overall well-being.

With these tested strategies in mind, let's think about how we can more consciously integrate the 3 C's into our daily routines and interactions. By bringing mindful awareness to our everyday actions and choices, we can create more opportunities for compassion, creativity, and connection to flourish in our lives.

First, you might want to think about your day from the moment you wake each day. What do you do first thing in the morning? Do you rush through your morning or take time to be kind to yourself? When you talk to your family or friends, are you listening to them or thinking about something else? Do you share your ideas and listen to theirs? Listening to our inner voice and others is how we purposefully build connections.

At work or school, when you have a project, do you decide to just get it out of the way, or do you try to make it something special? That's creativity.

Now, let's say you find out you're not doing these things as much as you want to. That's okay. You can set intentions to do better. Intentions are like promises to yourself. You decide, *"I will be kinder," "I will listen,"* or *"I will share my ideas."* It's not about being perfect right away. It's about trying a little more each day.

When you set these intentions, you'll want to write them down where you can see them, maybe on a note in your room or a reminder on your phone. It helps you remember what you're trying to do. Every time you see your promise, it's like a little nudge, reminding you to be kind, connect, and be creative.

These things make a big difference.

> *When you live with the 3 C's, you feel better. You make your friends and family feel good. You change the atmosphere to one that didn't exist before. And when things get tough, which is a "given," you have these 3 C's like tools to help you navigate the rough storms.*

Living in alignment with the 3 C's is something you do bit by bit. You look at what you're doing now and see where you can improve. You set your promise, and you try. And every time you try, you get closer to living the life you want -- a life filled with compassion, connections, and creativity. It's a big deal, but it starts with small steps.

As we explore how to integrate the 3 C's into our daily lives, I'm reminded of my own journey. Remember the stories I shared at the beginning of this book? I recounted my grandfather's compassionate lesson about borrowing money, the creative spark ignited by Louis Armstrong's trumpet playing, and my father's connection with the community through his "Officer Friendly" presentations. These were the seeds of transformation that have grown in me throughout my life.

Looking back, I can see how these experiences shaped my path. The compassion my grandfather showed me became a guiding principle in my interactions with others. The creativity inspired by Louis Armstrong fueled my passion for music and my belief in the power of artistic expression. And the connection my father fostered within our community inspired my commitment to building bridges and understanding between people.

These threads of compassion, creativity, and connection have been woven together to create the fabric of my life's work. From my career as a musician to my role as a minister, from my civic leadership to my advocacy for social justice, through all of this the 3 C's have been my constant companions and guides.

Your journey of integrating the 3 C's may look different from mine, but it can be equally transformative. As you continue to embody these principles, you will find, as I have, that they become more than practices. They become integral parts of who you are. They shape your decisions, your relationships, and your impact on the world around you.

Now, let's explore how we can deepen our understanding and practice of the 3 C's in our daily lives.

3 C's Mastery: Deepening Your Practice

Let's talk about growing and getting better at things that matter. When we think about compassion, connection, and creativity, there's always a little more we can learn. And that's exciting, right? Recognizing that the journey ahead is filled with opportunities to show compassion, you are ready to establish new connections and inspire innovative ideas.

As we dive deeper into integrating the 3 C's, it's worth recalling Dr. Kristin Neff's insights on self-compassion. Expanding on her earlier teachings, Neff emphasizes that compassion, like any skill, can be strengthened through regular practice. This applies not only to self-compassion but also to compassion for others, reinforcing the idea that continuous, intentional effort is key to embodying the compassionate aspect of our 3 C's framework.

We're moving into the heart of learning, which is how to improve compassion, make connections, and be creative. It's like going on a treasure hunt. But instead of looking for gold or jewels, we're looking for moments to be caring, and times to make new friends or support old ones, and ways to think up something that we believe no one has thought of before.

Now, think about how to get better at these things. It's like learning to ride a bike. At first, we might fall off a few times, but we keep going. And soon, we're zooming around like pros.

To practice compassion, I suggest that you start by noticing how you and those around you feel. When a friend is sad, what can you do? You might sit still or hug your friend. And the more you do it, the better you get.

To practice connection, talk and listen to people. It's like tossing a ball back and forth. You say something, then you listen to something said to you. When you listen, you make the other person feel important, and you learn a lot. You can practice this every day by asking someone about their day and carefully listening to their response, with a mind toward establishing a real connection.

Creativity is fun to practice. It's like playing with building blocks. You take an idea here and there and put it together in a new way. Try drawing a picture of something you've never seen or written about before. The more you play with ideas, the more creative you become.

It's clear that we're talking about a journey here. You're not looking to be perfect from day one, but to take little steps every day to get better. It's saying, *"I'm going to try being kinder today,"* or *"I'm going to make a new friend this week."* These simple gestures add up to something big.

And one more thing. It goes beyond you getting better. You're about making the world better, too. When we're kind, listen, and share our ideas, the world gets a little brighter. It's like each of us has a light inside, and every time we show compassion, make a new connection, or do something creative, our light shines brighter.

So, let's keep looking for chances to learn, practice, and grow. It's a path that never ends, and that's what makes it so wonderful. Every day is a new chance to shine.

Your 3 C's Mission Statement

Life often feels like a never-ending to-do list. But beyond the daily grind, what truly matters to you? Is it kindness, friendship, or creativity? These qualities align with your 3 C's and understanding what you value helps you make choices that resonate with your authentic self.

"Enter" the personal mission statement! What a powerful tool for purposeful living. Think of it as a map for your life's journey. You have a daily routine, but your actions align with your overall direction and purpose. Your mission statement captures the essence of who you are and who you want to become.

Why do you need one? Because life gets busy, and you might forget what's important. A mission statement helps you remember. It enables you to make choices that align with your core values. You look at your mission statement when you have to decide something, and it will guide you.

How do you make a mission statement? You think about the 3 C's, of course. How do these matter to you? First, think about compassion. How do you practice compassion toward yourself and others, taking action to alleviate suffering or meet needs and bring joy to another's life? Write down your ideas.

Next, think about connections. How do you build relationships with other people? Write these thoughts down, too. Finally, think about creativity. What you like to make or do for leisure or fun is what you put on paper.

When you're finished, look at what you wrote and pick out the most essential parts. These are the seeds of your mission statement.

Let's craft your mission statement, focusing on truly listening with purpose to the needs of others and taking meaningful actions to support and uplift their lives. Start with, *"I want to live a life where..."* Then, add your most important ideas. For example, *"I want to live a life where I am kind to everyone, build strong friendships, and create beautiful art."* This becomes your mission statement. It says what you want from life, and you can change it as you grow and learn.

Now, what do you do with it? Use it! When you wake up, read it. When you have to make a choice, think about it. Does this choice fit with your mission statement? If not, then think again. You want to make choices that fit with who you want to be.

Maybe you're thinking, *"But what if it's hard to stick to my mission statement?"* That's okay. It's not about being perfect. It's about trying your best. When you make a mistake, look at your mission statement and start again.

Remember, your mission statement is for you to make your life better. It is to help you live by the 3 C's. When you do, you'll feel good. You'll make a difference in the world.

3 C's-Friendly Environment

Your daily environments -- home, work, even places you shop or relax -- profoundly impact your life. They can elevate or deflate you. Creating spaces that nurture your growth is crucial. Surround yourself with people who understand and support you, who champion your success. It's like planting your personal growth in the richest soil that gives you the best chance to flourish.

Our old friend, Dr. Mihaly Csikszentmihalyi, has more wisdom to share with us. Remember how we talked about his work on flow and creativity? He also emphasizes how important our environment is for fostering creativity and well-being. Think about it. The space around you can either help you get into that flow state where you're fully immersed and enjoying what you're doing, or it can throw up roadblocks. So, when you're setting up your creative space, keep Csikszentmihalyi's insights in mind. Your environment could be the key to unlocking your creative potential!

Building your support network starts with who you let into your life. Look for friends who truly listen, who celebrate your wins, and stand by you in tough times. These are your cheerleaders, your go-to people when life gets rocky.

How do you find these folks? Start small. Take a look at your phone contacts. Who lights you up when you talk to them? These are your people. If your current circle isn't quite cutting it, then branch out. Join a club that matches your interests, or volunteer for a cause you care about. You'll meet like-minded people who share your values.

Never forget that nurturing connections is a two-way street. Be the friend you wish to have by listening without judgment, offering support, and celebrating others' successes. This creates a network that uplifts and fosters growth.

Are you ready to put this into action? Start small:

- Check your phone contacts to assess if frequent connections are supportive. If not, branch out to people and places that align with your interests. Be open and friendly; small steps lead to big changes.
- At home, create a personal nook. It needn't be large - just a corner for reading, creating, or pursuing what you love. This is your launchpad, your "mini oasis."
- Don't neglect your workspace. Personalize your desk with plants or meaningful photos. These touches, reminding you of the 3 C's, are beacons guiding you through challenges.
- Foster team spirit at work. Collaborate, share ideas, and celebrate collective wins, creating an environment where everyone can thrive and support each other's success.

One more thing. Take a look at your day. How do you spend your time? Are you running around, always busy? Take a step back. Make time for what matters -- the people and things that fill you up. Say "no" to everything that doesn't help you grow. Yes, this can be hard, but it's worth it.

Creating a supportive environment is a really big deal. It's not just knowing where you are. It's who you're with, how you feel, and what you do. It's a mix of people, places, and choices. And remember, it's not a race. It's a journey, so, take your time. Make choices that feel right for you. Bit by bit, you'll build a world around you that's all about compassion, connection, and creativity. That's the real secret to growth and it can all start today.

Think about it. Instead of overhauling your entire life overnight, what if you could plant seeds of compassion, nurture tiny sprouts of creativity, and cultivate little connections each day? These might seem insignificant at first, but just like a mighty oak growing from a small acorn, these tiny habits are sure to lead to profound changes with time.

This is where Dr. BJ Fogg's "Tiny Habits" method comes into play. Remember when we explored this approach in the context of self-care? Well, it turns out that this powerful tool isn't just great for taking care of ourselves; it's equally effective for integrating the 3 C's into our daily lives.

Tiny Habits, Big 3 C's Impact

Dr. Fogg's method consists of making small, manageable changes that gradually lead to significant transformations. Just as we applied it to self-care routines, we can use this approach to make lasting changes in our practice of compassion, creativity, and connection. The beauty of this method is that it makes the process of change feel less daunting and more achievable.

Dr. Fogg's research shows that big changes must essentially start with small steps. He suggests that instead of trying to make enormous leaps, we should focus on tiny, easy-to-do behaviors. These small actions, when done consistently, can snowball into very significant changes.

Here's how it works:

Choose a Tiny Behavior: Pick something so small you can't say "no." For compassion, it might be sending one kind text message a day. For connection, it could be smiling at one stranger each morning. For creativity, try doodling for just one minute.

Find an Anchor: Link your new tiny habit to something you already do. For example, *"After I brush my teeth, I will think of one thing I'm grateful for."*

Celebrate: This is so important! After you do your tiny habit, celebrate immediately. This could be as simple as saying, *"I did it!"* or doing a little dance. This positive emotion helps wire the new habit into your brain.

Dr. Fogg's "ABC" framework — Anchor, Behavior, Celebration — makes it easier to form new habits. By starting small and building on success, we can gradually incorporate more compassion, creativity, and connection into our daily lives.

3 C's in Tough Times

Sometimes, we find ourselves in environments that seem to work against compassion, creativity, and connection. But even in these challenging situations, it's possible to embody the 3 C's and create positive change.

A powerful example of this is the Circles of Support and Accountability (CoSA) program. CoSA works with high-risk offenders, particularly those convicted of sexual offenses, as they reintegrate into society. This might seem like the last place you'd find compassion, creativity, and connection, but CoSA proves otherwise.

Here's how CoSA embodies the 3 C's:

Compassion: CoSA volunteers show deep compassion by supporting individuals who are often shunned by society. They see the humanity in people who have made serious mistakes and offer them a chance at redemption.

Creativity: The program uses creative approaches to help offenders build new, positive lives. This might involve finding innovative ways to secure housing, employment, or healthy social connections.

Connection: At its core, CoSA builds connections. It creates a support network for the offender, fostering positive relationships that guide them toward a better path.

The results are remarkable. Studies have shown that CoSA significantly reduces re-offending rates. By integrating the 3 C's, even in this challenging environment, CoSA transforms lives and makes communities safer.

This example shows us that no matter where we are or what we're facing, we can practice compassion, tap into our creativity, and build meaningful connections. These principles will guide us in creating positive change, even in the most unlikely circumstances.

Celebrating Your 3 C's Journey

So, you've been walking this path for a while now. You've been working hard to study and reflect upon what makes life rich and rewarding. It's been a journey of embracing the 3 C's—compassion, connection, and creativity. And guess what? It's time to stop and celebrate. Yes, celebrate!

Dr. Robert Emmons, a leading gratitude researcher, has found that recognizing and appreciating our progress and achievements can significantly boost our well-being and motivation. Celebration is first of all, fun. It's also an integral part of our personal growth and continued success.

What's the point of growing if we don't take a moment to realize how far we've come? You see, acknowledging your growth is a major step leading to more growth, greater joy, and a bigger impact.

Let's break it down, shall we? We will discuss why celebrating your growth in embodying the 3 C's is a big deal. But, we'll also discuss in detail how you can do it because you deserve to recognize the good you've added to your life and the lives of others.

First, let's focus on you. Think back to when you began this journey. I know you remember the initial uncertainty, the struggle to be more compassionate, connected, and creative. Now look at you! You're a changed person. Perhaps you're more understanding and kind, both to others and to yourself. Maybe you're building relationships that are deep and true. Or you're finding that creativity is a way of solving problems and living. This change, this growth, it's worth recognizing.

Here's a formula that I've proven to be effective. Grab a pen and paper or open up a new document on your computer. Write down the changes you've seen in yourself. Be specific. Did you comfort a friend in a way you never could have before? Write it down. Did you connect with a stranger, sharing a surprisingly profound moment? Make a note of it. Did you find a creative solution to a problem at work that made everyone's lives easier? That's right, jot it down.

After you've made your list, take a moment. Breathe it in. This is your doing. Your commitment to the 3 C's has made these things happen. And when you celebrate these wins, no matter how small they may seem, you fuel your fire, which motivates you to keep going and growing.

Growth extends outward like ripples in a pond. Your compassion, connection, and creativity have a way of touching others and making their lives a little brighter. Someone smiled or felt seen or thought of a new way to approach a problem. The positive impact you have on others is a beautiful thing, worthy of celebrating.

How do you celebrate this? It's simpler than you might think. Start by recognizing the fact that every act of compassion, genuine conversation, and creative spark you've shared matters. It's changed things. You won't always see the full effect, but rest assured, it's there. Therefore, take a moment to feel proud that you're making a difference. Then, keep looking for ways to spread those powerful 3 C's. Keep the cycle of positivity going.

Here's a pro tip. Share your celebrations with someone. It multiplies the joy. Tell a friend about the progress you've made. Or better yet, celebrate their growth alongside your own. It strengthens your connections and spreads the very ideals you're embracing. Plus, it's just plain fun to celebrate together. You'll see.

To wrap this up, remember that celebrating your growth and impact isn't merely a nice thing to do. It's an essential part of the process. It helps you appreciate the journey, not just the destination. And it reminds you that what you're doing, this work of living by the 3 C's, is powerful. It's transforming your life and touching the lives of others.

So, go ahead, take the time to celebrate. You've earned it. And then, with a smile on your face and a heart full of joy, keep moving forward. Keep embodying compassion, connection, and creativity. The world needs more of it, and so do you.

3 C's Champions: Real-Life Success Stories

To truly understand the transformative power of integrating compassion, creativity, and connection, let's look at some inspiring examples:

The **Edible Schoolyard Project**, founded by Alice Waters, is a shining example of how the 3 C's can come together to create meaningful change. This organization integrates compassion for the environment and community, creativity in gardening and cooking, and connection with nature and local food systems. By teaching children to grow and prepare their own food, the Edible Schoolyard Project fosters a deep sense of responsibility, innovation, and community spirit. It demonstrates to us that when we combine the 3 C's, we can cultivate a generation that values sustainability and healthy living.

Another remarkable example is **Ashoka**, an organization that supports social entrepreneurs worldwide. Ashoka's mission is to foster compassion, creativity, and connection in addressing global challenges. By empowering individuals to develop innovative solutions to social problems, Ashoka creates a network of change makers who are driven by empathy and collaboration. This organization demonstrates that when we integrate the 3 C's, we can tackle complex issues and contribute to a more just and equitable world.

These examples remind us that the 3 C's are more than abstract concepts – they are powerful tools for creating positive change. By learning from these organizations and integrating compassion, creativity, and connection into our own lives, we significantly impact our communities and the world.

As we conclude our exploration of integrating and embodying the 3 C's, let's reflect upon the transformative journey we've undertaken. This is about understanding concepts, and then adapting them to our daily living. As Maya Angelou wisely said, *"Do the best you can until you know better. Then when you know better, do better."*

Throughout this chapter, we've delved into the practical application of Compassion, Creativity, and Connection in our daily lives. We've explored how these principles interweave to create a rich tapestry of personal growth and positive impact on the world around us.

REFLECTIONS - Chapter 12: Living the 3 C's

Integration Assessment:

1. How have you transformed through practicing the 3 C's?
2. Where do you see the biggest shifts in your daily life?
3. Which C has shown the most growth?
4. What resistance or challenges remain?
5. How are others responding to your changes?

3 C's Integration Tracker:

1. **Daily Practice Monitor** ▫ Morning 3 C's intention setting ▫ Mindful implementation moments ▫ Evening reflection on impact ▫ Opportunities recognized/taken
2. **Transformation Indicators** ▫ Compassion becoming automatic ▫ Creative solutions emerging naturally ▫ Deeper connections forming ▫ Integration of all 3 C's
3. **Ripple Effect Observer** ▫ Impact on relationships ▫ Influence on others ▫ Community changes ▫ Unexpected positive outcomes

Action Steps:

- Notice natural integration points
- Document synergies between C's
- Track compound effects
- Record breakthrough moments

REFLECTIONS - Chapter 12: Living the 3 C's

Integration Assessment:

Your 3 C's Transformation

As you integrate compassion, creativity, and connection into the fabric of your daily life, take time to acknowledge your growth and envision your continued evolution.

Reflection Prompts:

- How has your understanding of the 3 C's deepened?
- What surprised you most about this journey?
- Where do you see the greatest potential for further growth?
- How are you inspiring others through your practice?

Integration Insights:

- Most powerful lessons learned
- Favorite practices developed
- Challenges overcome
- New habits formed

Future Vision Setting: How will you continue to embody the 3 C's?

Compassion growth:_____

Creativity expansion: _____

Connection deepening: _____

Remember: Living the 3 C's is an ongoing journey of growth and impact. Your practice creates ripples that touch countless lives in ways you may never know.

What will be your legacy of Compassion, Creativity, and Connection?

COMING ATTRACTIONS

AN EXCLUSIVE ALL-ACCESS LOOK

behind the transformation that changed everything

THE 3 C's
TRANSFORMATION

PROGRESS &
PERSEVERANCE

Featuring Never-Before-Seen

EXCLUSIVE INSIGHTS
INTIMATE INTERVIEWS
TRANSFORMATION MOMENTS

Plus an exclusive first look at

LIFE AFTER THE 3 C's

"inspiring" • *"deeply reflective"* • *"the perfect bookend"*

CHAPTER 13

The story continues...

THE 3 C'S TRANSFORMATION: PROGRESS AND PERSEVERANCE

"I don't want my life to just happen. I want to happen to my life."
— Luke Perry

These powerful words, spoken to me by my dear friend and fellow cast mate, Luke Perry, during our time together on the ABC soap opera *Loving* in the late 1980s, have stayed with me throughout my journey. I can vividly recall the intensity in Luke's eyes as he shared this philosophy. It was more than a casual remark. It was a guiding principle that shone through in everything he did, both on and off-screen.

Luke's passion for living and a deep sense of purpose were infectious. He approached each day, each scene, and each interaction with an intentionality that was truly inspiring. Though he tragically left us too soon, the gift of his words continues to inspire and guide me, and I hope they will do the same for you.

"Lukester's" message about actively shaping our lives rather than passively letting them unfold perfectly encapsulates the journey we've been on throughout this book. As we have explored the transformative power of our 3 C's — Compassion, Creativity, and Connection — we've discovered how these fundamental principles help us live authentically, with purpose and intention.

In this final chapter, we'll bring together all that we've learned, seeing how the 3 C's intertwine to create a life of meaning, fulfillment, and positive impact. It's clear that these concepts have the power to dramatically change our individual lives and also our communities and the world.

Throughout this book, we've explored how cultivating compassion opens our hearts to others, how tapping into our creativity allows us to solve problems in innovative ways, and how fostering genuine connections enriches our lives and creates ripple effects of positive change.

Now, as we stand at the threshold of applying these principles in our daily lives, it's essential to understand that this isn't a journey toward perfection. It's all about progress. Every small act of kindness, every creative solution to a problem, every authentic connection we make become the building blocks of a more compassionate, creative, and connected world.

Remember Luke Perry's powerful words: *"I don't want my life to just happen. I want to happen to my life."* This is our call to action.

> By embracing the 3 C's, we're not passively letting life unfold around us. Instead, we're actively shaping our experiences, our relationships, and our impact on the world.

As you move forward from this book, I encourage you to look for opportunities to practice compassion, even in the smallest of ways. Be on the lookout for chances to apply your creativity, not just in your traditional "artistic" pursuits, but in how you approach challenges and interactions. And above all, nurture your connections with yourself first.

The journey of the 3 C's is ongoing. It's a path of continuous growth and discovery. But with each step you take, you're transforming your own life, and at the same time you're contributing to a global shift toward a better world. And that, dear reader, is how we truly "happen to our lives."

Luke Perry's words remind us that life isn't something that simply unfolds around us, but it's something we actively shape. With the 3 C's as our guide, we have the tools to craft a life of meaning and purpose. But knowledge alone isn't enough. As we near the end of our journey together, it's time to transform our understanding into action.

3 C's in Action: Your Next Steps

Now that we've explored the transformative power of compassion, creativity, and connection let's put these principles into action. Here are specific steps you can take to embody the 3 C's in your daily life. These steps helped me immensely when I was ready to take actionable steps.

Compassion in Action:

- Start each day with a loving-kindness meditation,

extending good wishes to yourself and others.

- Perform one random act of kindness daily, no

matter how small.

- Practice active listening in your conversations,

focusing on understanding rather than responding.

Cultivating Creativity:

- Set aside 15 minutes each day for a creative

activity, whether it's writing, drawing, or problem-solving.

- Challenge yourself to find a creative solution to a problem at work or at home each week.

- Engage in "possibility thinking" by asking *"What if?"* questions when faced with challenges.

Fostering Connection:

- Reach out to one person each day—a friend, family member, or colleague - to strengthen your relationships.

- Join or start a community group aligned with your interests or values.

- Practice vulnerability by sharing your thoughts and feelings more openly with trusted individuals.

Integrating the 3 C's:

- Create a "3 C's Moment" each day where you consciously combine all three principles into a single action or experience.

- Start a "3 C's Challenge" with friends or family where you collectively brainstorm ways to integrate the principles within your community.

- Reflect on your day each evening, identifying how
you employed the 3 C's separately and together.

Sustainable Practice:

- Design a personal ritual incorporating the 3 C's,
such as a morning gratitude practice that includes
visualization and reaching out to a loved one.
- Set up regular check-ins with yourself to assess
your progress, and adjust your approach to living
the 3 C's.
- Create a vision board that represents your "3 C's
life," and place it where you'll see it daily.

Remember, you're on an intentional journey where the "climb" is more relevant than the destination. Start small, be consistent, and watch as these practices transform your life and the lives of those around you. The power to create positive change lies within you—it's time to unleash it!

3 C's Future: A World Transformed

As we look to the future, you can now imagine a world where the 3 C's are embraced by individuals, communities, and societies-at-large. You now picture a society where:

Compassion guides our interactions, leading to reduced conflict, increased understanding, and a collective commitment to easing suffering. In schools, "empathy education" is as fundamental as math or science. In workplaces, success is measured, not just by profits but by a positive impact on employees' well-being.

Creativity is nurtured in all aspects of life, resulting in innovative solutions to global challenges, a renaissance in arts and culture, and a workforce equipped to adapt to rapid change. Cities are designed as living works of art, integrating nature and technology in beautiful, sustainable ways. Problem-solving think tanks bring together diverse minds to tackle issues, from climate change to social inequality, with fresh, imaginative approaches.

Connection is prioritized, fostering strong communities, bridging divides between different groups, and creating a global network of mutual support and understanding. Technology is used to bring people together rather than isolating them. Community centers become hubs of intergenerational learning and sharing. Global citizen exchange programs become as common as studying abroad.

In this world, the 3 C's aren't only personal practices but societal values that shape policy, education, and culture. Imagine walking down a street where strangers smile and greet each other, where public spaces are alive with creative expression, and where the sense of global interconnectedness is palpable in every interaction. That sounds fantastic because it is!

By manifesting the 3 C's in our daily lives, we're not just improving our own existence, we're contributing to this vision of a more compassionate, creative, and connected world. Every act of kindness, every creative solution, and every genuine connection ripples outward, influencing others and gradually reshaping our collective reality.

As you move forward from this book, please carry with you the knowledge that you have the power to create positive change. Together, we can build a future where compassion, creativity, and connection are the cornerstones of a thriving, harmonious world.

This vision of a transformed future is already taking shape in our individual lives and stories. Since unlocking the power of the 3 C's, you probably recognized how these principles have been at work in your own experiences. I've certainly seen their impact throughout my life journey.

As we conclude our exploration of the 3 C's, I'm reminded of how these principles have shaped my path. Remember the stories I shared at the beginning of this book? Here, once more, is my story:

Compassion: My grandfather's lesson about borrowing money wasn't just about financial responsibility. It was a profound act of compassion because he took the time to teach me by showing patience and understanding. This experience taught me that genuine compassion often involves empowering others.

Creativity: The moment I heard Louis Armstrong play his trumpet became a spark of pure creativity inside of me. It was the music, but it was also the power of creative expression to move and inspire. This experience showed me that creativity can be a bridge, connecting us to emotions and experiences beyond words.

Connection: My father's "Officer Friendly" presentations exemplified the power of connection. By using magic and humor, he built bridges between the police and the community. This taught me that genuine connection can transcend boundaries and create understanding where there was once fear or mistrust.

These personal anecdotes are my personal, living examples of how the 3 C's shapes our lives and the world around us. Whether it's through a grandfather's compassionate lesson, a musician's creative inspiration, or a police officer's innovative approach to community connection, the ideals of Compassion, Creativity, and Connection will always inspire lasting change.

Finally, let's take a moment to distill the wisdom we've gathered along the way. By reflecting on these key lessons, we will better understand how to apply the 3 C's in our own lives, creating our own stories of transformation.

Measuring Your 3 C's Growth

As we've journeyed through the world of the 3 C's, you've likely noticed changes in yourself. But how do you measure this growth? It's not as simple as stepping on a scale or marking your height on a wall.

Returning to Dr. Carol Dweck's influential work on growth mindset from Chapter 9, and resilience in Chapter 10, I believe you see its relevance to tracking your personal growth. Dr. Dweck's research suggests that monitoring our progress reinforces a growth mindset.

When we actively note our improvements, however small, we're providing concrete evidence that our efforts lead to growth. This awareness encourages us to keep pushing forward, creating a positive feedback loop that enhances our commitment to personal development across all aspects of the 3 C's.

Allow me to offer some proven ways to measure your growth, and feel free to operationalize any or all of these:

Compassion Journal: Each day, write down one act of kindness you performed or witnessed. Over time, you'll see a beautiful record of compassion growing before your eyes. You could take the additional step of rating your emotional response on a scale from 1 (lowest) to 10 (highest) to track the degree to which your capacity for empathy is expanding.

Connection Counter: Keep a tally of meaningful conversations you have over time. Aim to increase this number gradually. Also, noting the depth of these connections, rating them from 1 (lowest) to 10 (highest) or most authentic interactions.

Creativity Catalog: Document your creative ideas or projects and set a goal to add to this catalog regularly. Challenge yourself to find one creative solution to an everyday problem as often as you can and record the outcomes.

3 C's Integration Log: Maybe once a week, reflect on an experience where you combined all 3 C's. Describe how you applied each "C," and the impact it had.

Mindfulness Meter: Rate your daily awareness of opportunities to practice the 3 C's on a scale of 1-10. Watch this number increase as you become more attuned to these moments in your daily life.

Resilience Tracker: When faced with challenges, note how you used the 3 C's to overcome them. Rate the effectiveness of your approach and how it evolves.

Impact Assessment: Periodically, reflect on how your practice of the 3 C's has influenced your well-being in relationships and at work. Look for tangible examples of positive change.

The important thing in all of this is not your number rating but your observance of trends and improvements over time. It's like watching seeds grow in your garden. With care and attention, you'll see beautiful changes blooming in your life.

If you want even more of a command of the outcome of everything we're shared here, consider creating a "3 C's Growth Dashboard" where you can visually track the different metrics. This could be a simple spreadsheet, a bullet journal spread, or even a custom app.

The key is to make it engaging and easy to maintain, so you're motivated to keep tracking your progress.

Conquering 3 C's Challenges

Yes, witnessing positive changes within you and those around you is a wonderful affirmation. However, as you integrate the 3 C's into your life, you'll likely face problems. I know I did. So let's address some common obstacles, along with my proposed remedies:

Time Constraints: Practice "time tracking," as suggested by Dr. Laura Vanderkam. For a week, or just a few days, log your activities in 30-minute increments. You'll discover pockets of time you hadn't noticed before. Could your commute now become a time for creative thinking? Could your lunch break be an opportunity for connection? Identify these hidden moments and purposefully allocate them to nurturing the 3 C's.

Self-Doubt: Apply Dr. Kristin Neff's wisdom on self-compassion. When you feel inadequate or question your progress, pause and treat yourself with the same kindness you'd offer a friend. Say to yourself, *"This is a moment of difficulty. Many people struggle with this. How can I comfort and care for myself right now?"* Remember, self-compassion isn't self-indulgence; it's a powerful tool to foster resilience and growth.

Lack of Visible Results: Dr. Angela Duckworth's research on grit shows us that progress isn't always linear or immediately apparent. Set small, achievable goals and definitely celebrate minor victories. Keep a journal to track these small wins, and I am confident that over time, you'll see how these seemingly insignificant actions accumulate into meaningful change.

Overwhelm: Break down the 3 C's into smaller, manageable actions. If practicing compassion feels daunting, start with a simple daily gratitude practice. If enhancing creativity seems overwhelming, begin with a five-minute daily free-writing exercise. For connection, set a goal to have one meaningful conversation each day. I keep saying this, but small, consistent actions lead to significant transformations.

Fear of Vulnerability: Recall Brené Brown's research on the power of vulnerability. Start small by sharing a personal story with a trusted friend or expressing appreciation to a colleague. As you practice opening up, you'll find that vulnerability isn't a weakness; it's the birthplace of innovation, creativity, and meaningful connections.

By addressing these obstacles head-on with specific strategies, you'll be better equipped to overcome them and continue your journey with the 3 C's. Remember, challenges are not roadblocks, but opportunities for growth and deeper integration of compassion, creativity, and connection in your life.

3 C's Everywhere: Adapting to Any Situation

The 3 C's can be applied anywhere, but their manifestation may vary depending on your environment. Consider these adaptations:

Work Environment: In a competitive workplace, practicing compassion might mean offering support to a stressed colleague. Creativity could involve finding one innovative solution to **a** work problem.

Family Life: Connection might mean having device-free dinners to encourage conversation. Compassion could involve really listening without judgment to a family member's concerns.

Community Involvement: Creativity could shine through organizing a neighborhood event. Compassion and connection might come together as you volunteer for a local cause.

Remember Dr. Adam Grant's research on seeking feedback. His work also emphasizes the importance of being a "giver" in various contexts.

This aligns beautifully with our 3 C's approach. Just as seeking feedback helps us grow, being a giver allows us to practice compassion, foster connections, and creatively contribute to others' lives. It's another powerful way to embody the 3 C's in different areas of our lives.

Celebrating 3 C's Victories

Recall Dr. Teresa Amabile's research in Chapter 10 about the power of progress. She reminds us that recognizing even small steps forward can significantly boost our motivation and happiness.

In the context of our 3 C's journey, this means taking time to appreciate how you've grown in compassion, creativity, and connection.

Here are some milestones that I suggest you celebrate:

Compassion: Celebrate after the first time you notice yourself automatically responding with kindness when you previously might have been impatient.

Connection: Celebrate when you've formed a new, meaningful relationship or deepened an existing one.

Creativity: Celebrate the moment you complete a creative project or implement an innovative idea.

Celebration doesn't have to be grand. It could be as simple as treating yourself to your favorite dessert or sharing your achievement with a friend. In all scenarios, you are acknowledging how far you've come and motivating yourself to keep growing.

3 C's for Life: Your Ongoing Journey

The journey of integrating the 3 C's into your life is ongoing. There's always more to learn and more ways to grow. Dr. Carol Dweck's work on growth mindset is particularly relevant here. Consider your difficulties to be opportunities to develop your compassion, connection, and creativity further.

Every step forward is a victory worth celebrating. Make the 3 C's a part of your daily routine. Here are even more strategies to ensure your continuous growth:

Read Widely: Expose yourself to diverse perspectives and ideas.

Seek Feedback: Ask trusted friends or mentors how they perceive your growth in the 3 C's.

Try New Things: Regularly step out of your comfort zone to stretch your capabilities.

As we conclude our exploration of the transformative power of the 3 C's, let's take a moment to reflect on the incredible journey we've undertaken together. This isn't the end of our path but the beginning of a lifelong adventure in personal growth and positive impact. Always be sure that you are the active, not the passive participant in your life.

REFLECTIONS

How have you seen the 3 C's transform your life since beginning this journey? Can you quantify your biggest challenge in implementing the 3 C's, and explain how you overcame it?

In what ways have you noticed your practice of the 3 C's influencing others around you? If so, you know that this is a really big deal! What legacy do you hope to create through your commitment to the 3 C's?

Practice Challenges: This week, while my book is fresh in your mind, challenge yourself to do these concrete things:

Compassion: Implement a daily compassion meditation practice.

Creativity: Apply a creative solution to a longstanding problem in your life or community.

Connection: Deepen a relationship by having a vulnerable, authentic conversation.

Embrace these opportunities with an open heart and mind, knowing that each small action contributes to a larger transformation.

"You got this!"

AND ...... CUT!

THAT'S A WRAP ON THE 3 C'S JOURNEY!

Ladies and gentlemen, as the credits roll on this transformative journey through The 3 C's, I hope you've enjoyed the show of a lifetime, particularly its lead character -- YOU!

From the pilot of The 3 C's Revolution to grand finale of The 3 C's Transformation, you've laughed, maybe you've cried, you've definitely engaged in thoughtful introspection and grown in ways you never imagined. As you step back into your daily life, give yourself a big hug because you're the star, the director, and the producer of your own 3 C's blockbuster.

The skills you've gained, the insights you've uncovered, and the transformations you've undergone comprise your toolkit for creating a life filled with Compassion, Creativity, and Connection.

But here's the real showstopper - your journey doesn't end when you close this book. The ripple effect of your transformation is just beginning. With the very next initiative that you take to live out the 3 C's, you'll inspire spin-offs all around you, turning your personal growth into a cultural phenomenon.

So, ending on the theatrical note because I love good theatre, as we dim the lights on this production after we've taken a bow and received a standing ovation, we know that the most exciting scenes are yet to be written and acted out. Your 3 C's journey is renewed for a lifetime of seasons, and I certainly can't wait to see what you'll create next. We'll all stay tuned, keep shining, and never stop rolling on our 3 C's adventures!

I feel compelled to formally invite you to join the "3 C's Movement. Yes, it has the strength of a Movement that will endure. This is your invitation to be part of something that goes beyond the pages of this book.

Once you're comfortable with the kinds and duration of your transformation, it's time to take your transformation out into the world and share what you've learned.

You can use your social media presence to let the everyone within your sphere of influence know that this very special change is possible! Join communities of like-minded individuals, and volunteer or mentor someone.

Be the spark that ignites change in others. The world needs more of the 3 C's, which means it needs more people like you.

Visit my website at www.billcmyers.com. There, you'll find a treasure trove of resources, including more book recommendations, information about workshops, private coaching, courses, and links to online communities. It's a place where you can connect with others on the same journey as you are on.

Don't be afraid to be vulnerable. Share your stories, your wins, your struggles in small spaces and public places. I'm cheering you on every step of the way, and you're cheering someone else on! The 3 C's are your ever-present, highly visible roadmap to transformative change.

.   .   .

Your light, when joined with others, has the power to illuminate the world. The journey of a thousand miles begins with a single step, and you've just taken that step. And you already know that you're not alone. Millions of others are walking alongside you, each in their own way.

The time is now. The visionary, the leader, the star are all synonyms for you. Let your journey with the 3 C's commence!

REFERENCES

Brown, B. (2012). Daring Greatly: How the Courage to Be Vulnerable Transforms the Way We Live, Love, Parent, and Lead. Gotham Books.

Csikszentmihalyi, M. (1990). Flow: The Psychology of Optimal Experience. Harper & Row.

Damon, W. (2008). The Path to Purpose: How Young People Find Their Calling in Life. Free Press.

Duckworth, A. (2016). Grit: The Power of Passion and Perseverance. Scribner.

Emmons, R. A. (2007). Thanks! How the New Science of Gratitude Can Make You Happier. Houghton Mifflin.

Eurich, T. (2017). Insight: Why We're Not as Self-Aware as We Think, and How Seeing Ourselves Clearly Helps Us Succeed at Work and in Life. Crown Business.

Frankl, V. E. (1959). Man's Search for Meaning. Beacon Press.

Fredrickson, B. L. (2009). Positivity: Top-Notch Research Reveals the 3-to-1 Ratio That Will Change Your Life. Crown Archetype.

Goleman, D. (1995). Emotional Intelligence: Why It Can Matter More Than IQ. Bantam Books.

Kabat-Zinn, J. (1990). Full Catastrophe Living: Using the Wisdom of Your Body and Mind to Face Stress, Pain, and Illness. Delacorte Press.

Kaufman, S. B. (2020). Transcend: The New Science of Self-Actualization. TarcherPerigee.

Kegan, R. (1982). The Evolving Self: Problem and Process in Human Development. Harvard University Press.

Koelsch, S. (2012). Brain and Music. Wiley-Blackwell.

Locke, E. A., & Latham, G. P. (1990). A Theory of Goal Setting and Task Performance. Prentice Hall.

Neff, K. (2011). Self-Compassion: The Proven Power of Being Kind to Yourself. William Morrow.

Riess, H. (2018). The Empathy Effect: Seven Neuroscience-Based Keys for Transforming the Way We Live, Love, Work, and Connect Across Differences. Sounds True.

Seligman, M. E. P. (2002). Authentic Happiness: Using the New Positive Psychology to Realize Your Potential for Lasting Fulfillment. Free Press.

Singer, T., & Klimecki, O. M. (2014). Empathy and compassion. Current Biology, 24(18), R875-R878.

Ungunmerr-Baumann, M. R. (2002). Dadirri: Inner Deep Listening and Quiet Still Awareness. In The Spirituality of the Earth (pp.34-37) Earthsong.

LET'S STAY CONNECTED
JOIN THE 3 C'S MOVEMENT

From the bottom of my heart, thank you for investing in this book and dedicating your valuable time to explore the Transformative Power of the 3 C's.

What an incredible journey we've been on! I'm thrilled to continue supporting your path of Compassion, Creativity, and Connection.

I'm available for:

- Workshops
- Speaking engagements
- One-on-one coaching
- Group coaching
- And more!

Visit me at www.billcmyers.com to learn more and access valuable resources. Don't forget to subscribe to stay updated on the latest 3 C's insights, opportunities and exciting new offerings!

For quick access to all my platforms, scan this QR code:

Let's stay connected on social media!

Share your 3 C's experiences using:

#3CsTransformation, #CompassionInAction, #CreativityUnleashed, and #ConnectionMatters.

Your stories inspire our community and might shape future books!

Remember, every small act of Compassion, burst of Creativity, or moment of Connection creates a ripple effect, transforming not just your life but the world around you. You've got this, and I'm here to support you.

I'm excited to continue this 3 C's revolution with you. Together, we're creating meaningful, positive change.

Transform yourself. Transform the world.

Let's make it happen!

With gratitude and excitement,

Bill

P.S. Scan that QR code and subscribe on the website - let's keep the 3 C's momentum going strong!